Guy's SCALES MODES & ARPEGGIOS

Created by Guy McRoskey

ISBN 978-0-615-26203-1 © 2009 Guy's Publishing Group, LLC. All rights reserved.

To Matthew and Jack

TABLE OF CONTENTS

Introduction 6

Major Scale and Its Modes

The Major Scale 12
The Dorian Scale 14
The Phrygian Scale 16
The Lydian Scale 18
The Mixolydian Scale 20
The Natural Minor Scale 22
The Locrian Scale 24

Harmonic Minor Scale and Its Modes

The Harmonic Minor Scale 26
The Locrian ♮6 Scale 28
The Ionian ♯5 Scale 30
The Dorian ♯4 Scale 32
The Phrygian Dominant Scale 34
The Lydian ♯2 Scale 36
The Superlocrian ♭7 Scale 38

Melodic Minor Scale and Its Modes

The Melodic Minor Scale 40
The Dorian ♭2 Scale 42
The Lydian Augmented Scale 44
The Lydian ♭7 Scale 46
The Mixolydian ♭6 Scale 48
The Locrian ♮2 Scale 50
The Altered Scale 52

Pentatonic and Blues Scales

The Major Pentatonic Scale 54
The Major Blues Scale 56
The Minor Pentatonic Scale 58
The Minor Blues Scale 60

Diminished and Whole Tone Scales

The Dominant Diminished Scale 62
The Diminished Scale 64
The Whole Tone Scale 66

Appendix: Triad Studies

Major Triad Study A-1
Minor Triad Study A-2
Diminished Triad Study A-3
Augmented Triad Study A-4
Sus2 Chords A-5
Sus4 Chords A-6

Playing a solo is like painting details over the backdrop of a scenic mural. For the soloist, the backdrop is a particular chord progression, over which the soloist enjoys great liberty to "paint" as he or she pleases. But, that liberty has certain boundaries. The soloist, like the painter, must learn to "paint" skillfully. That skill requires a strong working knowledge of scales and arpeggios. This book provides the basis for developing that knowledge.

Whole Steps and Half Steps

The *musical alphabet* of the Western musical tradition consists of seven letters — A, B, C, D, E, F, and G — plus five additional notes called *accidentals*, for a total of twelve notes. The letters correspond to the notes played on the white keys of a piano. The black keys on the piano are the accidentals, which fall between the adjacent white-key notes. For example, the black key to the right of an "A" note is higher in pitch than the "A" but lower in pitch than the "B," and is referred to as either "A#" (pronounced "A sharp") or "B♭" (pronounced "B flat"). Movement to an adjacent piano key (black or white) is referred to as a "*semitone*" or "*half step*" ("H"). Movement to a piano key (black or white) that is one beyond the adjacent key is referred to as a "*tone*" or "*whole step*" ("W"). On the guitar, a span of one fret comprises the half-step interval and a span of two frets comprises the whole-step interval, as illustrated below — with maroon dots (●) depicting finger placement.

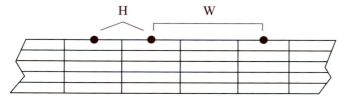

Figure 1: Half Steps and Whole Steps on the Fretboards

Scales

A *scale* is a sequence of notes arranged with reference to a starting note called the "*tonic*" — depicted graphically in this book by a blue square (■). Most scales have five to eight notes. Each scale has its own distinct *interval formula*, and can be described as a pattern of steps (e.g., half steps, whole steps, and combination whole-half steps). A scale that conforms to its interval formula without alteration is said to be *diatonic*. The diatonic C Major scale has the following notes: C-D-E-F-G-A-B (with C being the tonic). All Major scales follow the same interval formula: W-W-H-W-W-W-H. Furthermore, the scale tones of the Major scale are numbered (1, 2, 3, 4, 5, 6, and 7), and these numbers are referred to as *scale degrees*. Scales are commonly presented with the tonic being repeated as the 8th note — called the *octave* (from the Latin word for eight) — as shown below:

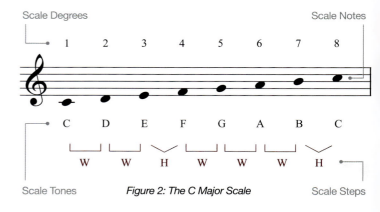

Figure 2: The C Major Scale

Intervals

Any two musical notes form an *interval*, which refers to the musical space or distance between the notes. The *quantity* of the interval refers to the number of scale tones in the interval, determined as follows:

1. The note having the lower frequency is identified and referred to as the "lower note." (If the two notes are identical, either note can serve as the lower note for this purpose.) The other note is referred to as the "higher note."

2. A major scale is constructed with the lower note as the tonic note. I will refer to this as the "reference scale."

3. The number of notes within the subject interval is counted this way:

    a. The counting begins with the tonic note of the reference scale (which counts as "one").

    b. The counting continues with the notes being counted as they appear sequentially in the reference scale.

    c. The counting ends with the counting of the higher note (which higher note may be found in a sharped or flatted condition in the reference scale).

4. The interval quantity refers to the number of notes so counted, as illustrated below:

Lower Note	Higher Note	Counting of Notes	Interval Quantity
C	G	1-2-3-4-5 C, D, E, F, G	5th
D	F	1-2-3 D, E, F#	3rd
B♭	A♭	1-2-3-4-5-6-7 B♭, C, D, E♭, F, G, A	7th

©2009 Guy's Publishing Group, LLC

The basic intervals are the Unison, 2nd, 3rd, 4th, 5th, 6th, 7th, and Octave. Intervals extending beyond an Octave are called *Compound Intervals*. Common examples are the 9th (Octave plus 2nd), 11th (Octave plus 4th) and 13th (Octave plus 6th).

Interval quality refers to the additional information conveyed by describing the interval quantity as "major," "minor," "perfect," "augmented," or "diminished." The rules for using these descriptive terms are as follows:

Intervals of 2nd, 3rd, 6th, and 7th

1. If the upper note is in the diatonic Major scale of the lower note, the correct descriptive term is "major" (e.g., major 3rd).
2. If the upper note is one half-step below a major interval, the correct descriptive term is "minor" (e.g., minor 3rd).
3. If the upper note is one half-step below a minor interval, the correct descriptive term is "diminished" (e.g., diminished 7th).
4. If the upper note is one half-step above a major interval, the correct descriptive term is "augmented" (e.g., augmented 2nd).

Intervals of Unison, Octave, 4th, and 5th

1. If the upper note is in the diatonic Major scale of the lower note, the correct descriptive term is "perfect" (e.g., perfect 5th).[1]
2. If the upper note is one half-step below a perfect interval, the correct descriptive term is "diminished" (e.g., diminished 5th).
3. If the upper note is one half-step above a major interval, the correct descriptive term is "augmented" (e.g., augmented 5th).

The intervals of the C Major scale are shown below:

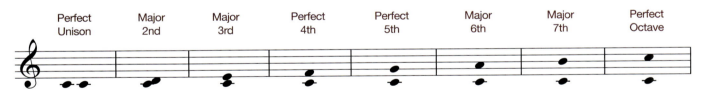

Figure 3: Intervals of the C Major Scale

Scale Formula

A Scale Formula describes the scale degrees in a particular scale, by reference to the diatonic Major scale (1-2-3-4-5-6-7). For example, the Mixolydian scale formula is 1-2-3-4-5-6-♭7. This formula tells us that the Mixolydian scale is identical to the Major scale, except that the 7th scale degree of the Mixolydian scale is flatted. That is to say, if you start with the Major scale and flat its 7th scale degree (i.e., move it one half step lower), the resulting scale is the Mixolydian scale. Scale formulas are utilized throughout this book.

Triads

1. A Triad is a three-note chord that can be stacked in thirds. When so stacked, the lowest note is called the root, the middle note is called the 3rd, and the highest note is called the 5th. In the C Major triad — spelled C-E-G — the C is the root, the E is the 3rd, and the G is the 5th.

2. The interval from the root to the 3rd may be a major third or a minor third. Likewise, the interval from the 3rd to the 5th may be a major third or a minor third. This means that the interval between the root and the 5th can be a perfect, diminished, or augmented fifth. Accordingly, there are four triad possibilities, as shown below:

Triad Name	Interval between Root & 3rd	Interval between Root & 5th	Scale Symbol for Triad
Major Triad	Major	Perfect	1, 3, 5
Minor Triad	Minor	Perfect	1, ♭3, 5
Diminished Triad	Minor	Diminished	1, ♭3, ♭5
Augmented Triad	Major	Augmented	1, 3, ♯5

3. When a triad is structured such that the 3rd tone is the *bass note* (i.e., the lowest tone in the chord), the chord is referred to as a *first-inversion* triad. Accordingly, when a C Major chord is played with an E in the bass, this is referred to as a first-inversion C chord.

4. When a triad is structured with the 5th note in the bass, the chord is referred to as a *second-inversion* triad. Accordingly, when a C Major chord is played with a G in the bass, this is referred to as a second-inversion C chord.

5. Two important variations on the Major triad are the sus2 chord and the sus4 chord. The sus2 chord is formed by lowering the 3rd of the Major triad by a whole step (scale symbol: 1, 2, 5). The sus4 chord is formed by raising the 3rd of the Major triad by a half step (scale symbol: 1, 4, 5).

[1] *Perfect intervals are special because of the mathematical ratio of the frequencies of the interval notes: Unison (1:1), Octave (2:1), 4th (4:3), and 5th (3:2).*

6. Because of the critical importance of triads to the scales found in this book, a triad study has been included in the Appendix. The triad study includes the sus2 and sus4 triads,[2] as they are important alterations of the Major triad.

Arpeggios

Playing certain notes of a scale simultaneously produces a *chord*, whereas playing the notes of a chord individually produces an arpeggio. In this book, emphasis is placed on chords and arpeggios formulated with the 1, 3, 5, and 7 scale degrees and their alterations in relation to the diatonic Major scale.

Modes

Every scale is named after its tonic note. Accordingly, the C Major scale is named after its tonic (C) and is played starting on that note. However, an interesting thing happens when the same C scale tones are played in order, but starting from a note other than C. If, for example, you start with the D (the second scale tone of the C Major scale), a step pattern is encountered that does not conform to the Major scale step pattern. This scale is known as the *Dorian scale* or the *Dorian mode* (and more precisely, *D Dorian* scale or mode — as the scale begins on the note D). For

The Phrygian scale is the third mode of the Major scale. Continuing with this exercise, we can see that there are seven modes for any diatonic scale — the parent scale and six other modes beginning on the notes other than the tonic of the parent scale.

This discovery is really very good news. The reason is, once you have learned a parent scale fingering pattern, the same pattern can be used with a different starting note to play the other modes of the parent scale. And, as it turns out, many of these modes are essential to the soloist — including the Natural Minor scale (the 6th mode of the major scale) and the Mixolydian scale (the 5th mode of the major scale). This book presents three important parent scales (and their modes): the Major scale, the Harmonic Minor scale, and the Melodic Minor scale.

Harmonized Scales

1. Harmonizing a scale means building chords using only the notes in that scale. The result is called a harmonized scale. Any scale can be harmonized. For example, if we use the C Major scale and build chords from only those notes in the C Major scale, the result is the C harmonized scale. Harmonized scales are an important concept for understanding chord progressions in all types of music.

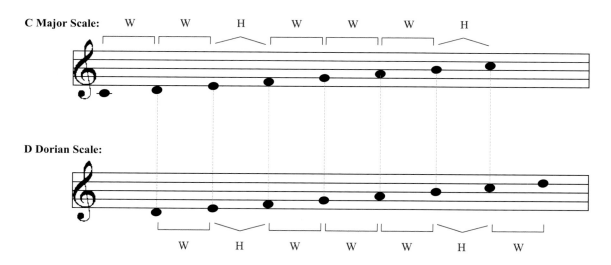

Figure 4: C Major and D Dorian Scales

this reason, the Dorian scale (or mode) is called the second mode of the Major scale. To generalize: a mode (e.g., D Dorian) is simply a scale having the same notes as a "parent" scale (e.g., C Major) but starting on a note other than the tonic note of the parent scale.

If we started on the E (the third scale tone of the C Major scale), the result is yet another scale/mode — called the Phrygian scale.

[2] *This book refers to the three-note sus2 and sus4 chords as triads, even though they do not technically satisfy the definition recited above.*

2. Most commonly, the harmonized scale is presented with the chords being constructed as "7th" chords built as a "stack of thirds." For illustration, the C Major scale is harmonized as such:

   - The first chord of the C Major harmonized scale is Cmaj7:
     C – the starting point (called the root)
     E – the note in the scale that is a third away from C
     G – the note in the scale that is a third away from E
     B – the note in the scale that is a third away from G

- The second chord of the C Major harmonized scale is Dm7:
  D – the root
  F – the note in the scale that is a third away from D
  A – the note in the scale that is a third away from F
  C – the note in the scale that is a third away from A

- The third chord of the C Major harmonized scale is Em7:
  E – the root
  G – the note in the scale that is a third away from E
  B – the note in the scale that is a third away from G
  D – the note in the scale that is a third away from B

- The fourth chord of the C Major harmonized scale is Fmaj7:
  F – the root
  A – the note in the scale that is a third away from F
  C – the note in the scale that is a third away from A
  E – the note in the scale that is a third away from C

- The fifth chord of the C Major harmonized scale is G7:
  G – the root
  B – the note in the scale that is a third away from G
  D – the note in the scale that is a third away from B
  F – the note in the scale that is a third away from D

- The sixth chord of the C Major harmonized scale is Am7:
  A – the root
  C – the note in the scale that is a third away from A
  E – the note in the scale that is a third away from C
  G – the note in the scale that is a third away from E

- The seventh chord of the C Major harmonized scale is Bm7(♭5):
  B – the root
  D – the note in the scale that is a third away from B
  F – the note in the scale that is a third away from D
  A – the note in the scale that is a third away from F

3. Because the intervals of the major scale are fixed, the harmonized major scale contains the same chord types in the same sequential order — regardless of the key. Compare, for example, the harmonized C Major scale and the harmonized G Major scale:

Cmaj7	Dm7	Em7	Fmaj7	G7	Am7	Bm7(♭5)
Gmaj7	Am7	Bm7	Cmaj7	D7	Em7	F♯m7(♭5)

Notice that the first chord for both scales is a maj7 chord, the second chord is a m7 chord, etc.

4. The chords of a harmonized scale are commonly referred to by number. To differentiate from scale degrees, the numbering of chords is done with Roman numerals. Moreover, upper-case (e.g., I, II, III, IV, etc.) is generally used for chords built from a major triad, and lower-case (e.g., i, ii, iii, iv, etc.) is generally used for chords built with either a minor or a diminished triad. Using this convention, the harmonized major scale is depicted generically as follows:

The Harmonized Major Scale

Imaj7	iim7	iiim7	IVmaj7	V7	vim7	viim7(♭5)

5. The numbering of other harmonized scales follows one of two conventions – which I refer to as the *intrinsic* and the *extrinsic* numbering systems. These two approaches are shown below with reference to the Dorian scale:

The Harmonized Dorian Scale – Intrinsic Numbering System

im7	iim7	IIImaj7	IV7	vm7	vim7(♭5)	VIImaj7

The Harmonized Dorian Scale – Extrinsic Numbering System

im7	iim7	♭IIImaj7	IV7	vm7	vim7(♭5)	♭VIImaj7

Notice the different designation of the third and seventh chords. According to the intrinsic numbering system, none of the chords are flatted or sharped. This reflects the fact that the chords are diatonic to the Dorian harmonized scale. However, according to the extrinsic numbering system, the third and seventh chords are both shown as flatted. This reflects the fact that the root of the chord is flatted as compared to the major scale. The modern trend is to utilize the extrinsic numbering system, and that system is used in this book.

Scale Relationships

An important part of learning scales is gaining an understanding of certain relationships between scales. The relationship of a parent scale and its derivative modes has already been discussed above. Other scale relationships to understand include the following:

- All of the scale and arpeggio patterns in this book are moveable. The key is to line up the pattern such that the tonic note is in the correct position. This concept is illustrated for the key of F major at the bottom of page 11.

- The Major Pentatonic and Minor Pentatonic scales share the same fingering patterns — the difference being the tonic note.

- Adding one note to the Minor Pentatonic scale produces the Minor Blues scale.
- Adding one note to the Major Pentatonic scale produces the Major Blues scale.
- The Natural Minor scale, the Harmonic Minor scale, and the Melodic Minor scale are closely related — differing only with regard to their 6th and 7th degrees.
- The Major scale and the Mixolydian scale differ only with regard to their 7th degree.
- The Diminished scale and the Dominant Diminished scales share the same fingering patterns — with the difference being the first step (whole step vs. half step).
- The Melodic Minor scale (ascending) and the Major scale differ only in their 3rd degree.

Numbering of Scale Patterns

In this book, the various fingering patterns for each scale are categorized according to a numbering system graphically depicted on the following page. This same numbering system is used (with a slight modification) to categorize moveable chords in a companion book, entitled, "Guy's Grids: More than a Chordbook" (see the inside of the back cover of this book).

How to Use this Book

First, don't be overwhelmed by this book. Mastering scales is a long-term endeavor. Here are some practical tips:

1. Practice scales and arpeggios for relatively short periods of time — but on a regular basis.
2. Practice with a purpose. Know before you start what your objective is for the practice session.
3. Use backing tracks frequently — whether you are doing scale and arpeggio exercises, practicing licks, or improvising. That makes the practice more fun, and gets you accustomed to playing with others.
4. Learn the more useful scales first. This means starting with the Major scale and the Harmonic Minor and Natural Minor scales, as well as the two Pentatonic scales (major and minor). Likewise, don't bother with the more exotic scales until you have a need or a particular desire to learn them. These more exotic scales include certain modes of the harmonic minor scale (the second, third, fourth, sixth, and seventh) and melodic minor scale (the second, third, and fifth).
5. Learn the most comfortable scale patterns first. But, don't work yourself into a rut only knowing one or two patterns.
6. When working with a particular scale pattern, also take the time to work with the related arpeggio pattern and chord. This integrated approach will pay great dividends in the long run.
7. Practice various scale sequences. One of my favorites involves playing an ascending sequence of thirds as follows: 1-3 | 2-4 | 3-5 | 4-6 | 5-7 | …and then playing a descending sequence of thirds as follows: 7-5 | 6-4 | 5-3 | 4-2 | 3-1 | ….
8. When learning a new guitar lick, alternate between playing the lick and playing the related scale and arpeggio patterns. This will help to associate the lick with the scale and arpeggio, and will make the lick that much more familiar and usable in improvisation.

Lastly, don't give up. Remember that even the longest journey begins with the first few steps. So, get started and stay with it. Those who persevere gain an awesome advantage. Enjoy!

Numbering of Scale Patterns

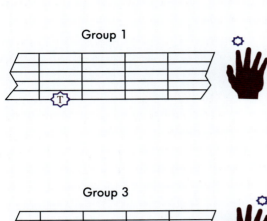
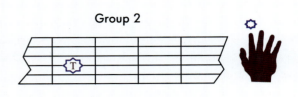
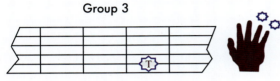
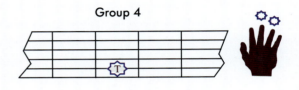
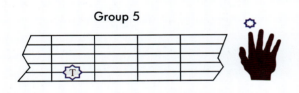
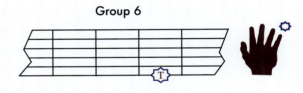
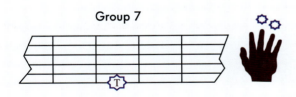

* *Combination of finger and string playing the tonic note (T).*

Using this numbering system, the F major scale patterns are categorized as follows:

Group 1:
The index finger plays the tonic note (F) on the 6th string, 1st fret.

Group 2:
The index finger plays the tonic note (F) on the 4th string, 3rd fret.

Group 3:
The pinky finger plays the tonic note (F) on the 5th string, 8th fret.

Group 4:
The middle finger plays the tonic note (F) on the 5th string, 8th fret.

Group 5:
The index finger plays the tonic note (F) on the 5th string, 8th fret.

Group 6:
The pinky finger plays the tonic note (F) on the 6th string, 13th fret.

Group 7:
The middle finger plays the tonic note (F) on the 6th string, 13th fret.

First Mode of Major Scale: Ionian Mode

The Major Scale

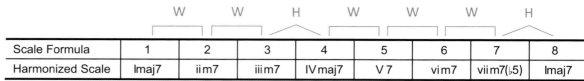
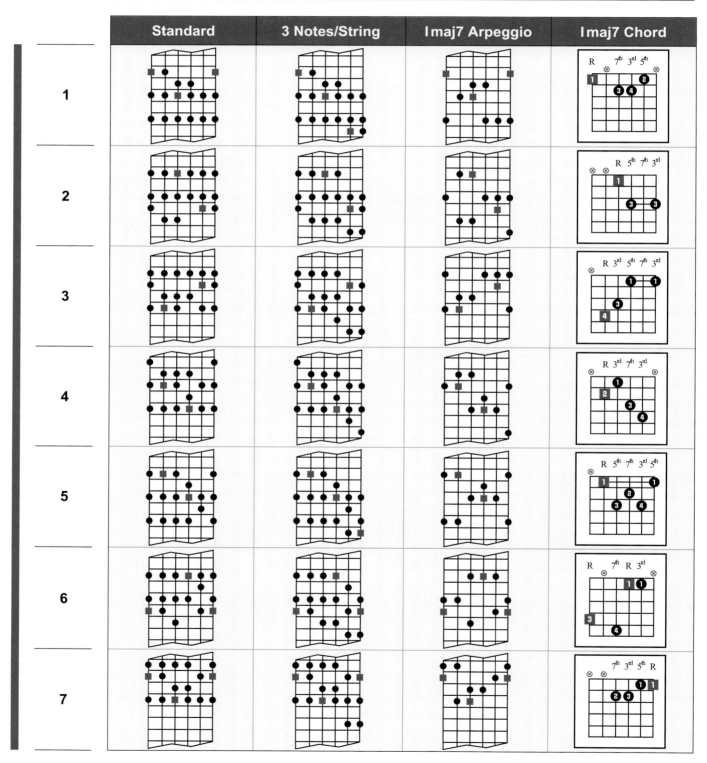

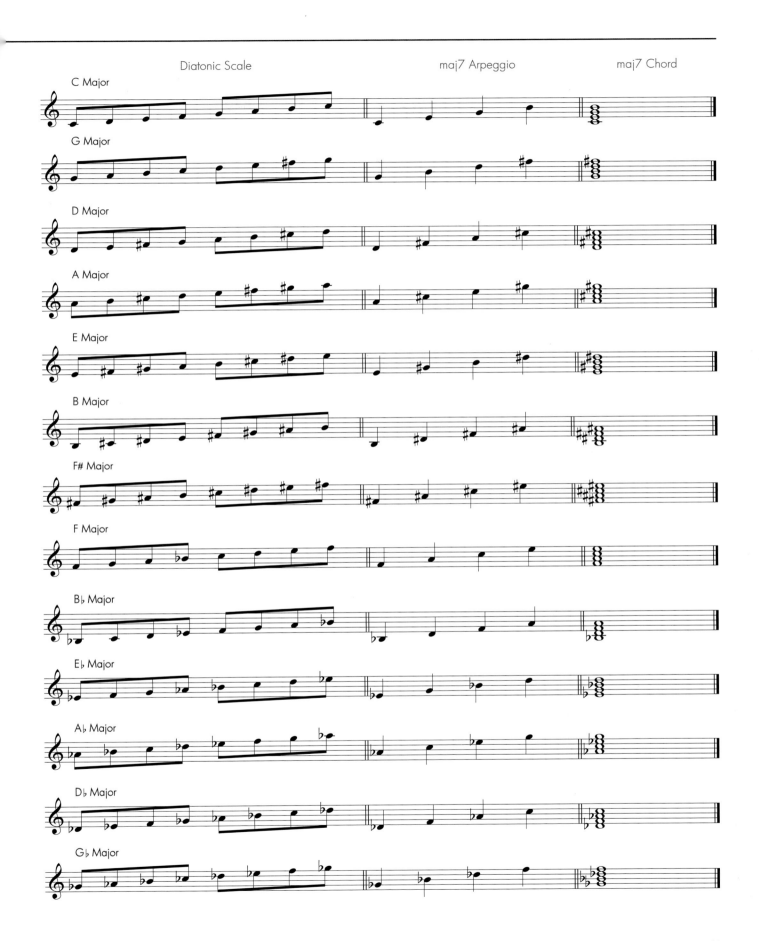

Second Mode of Major Scale: Dorian Mode
The Dorian Scale

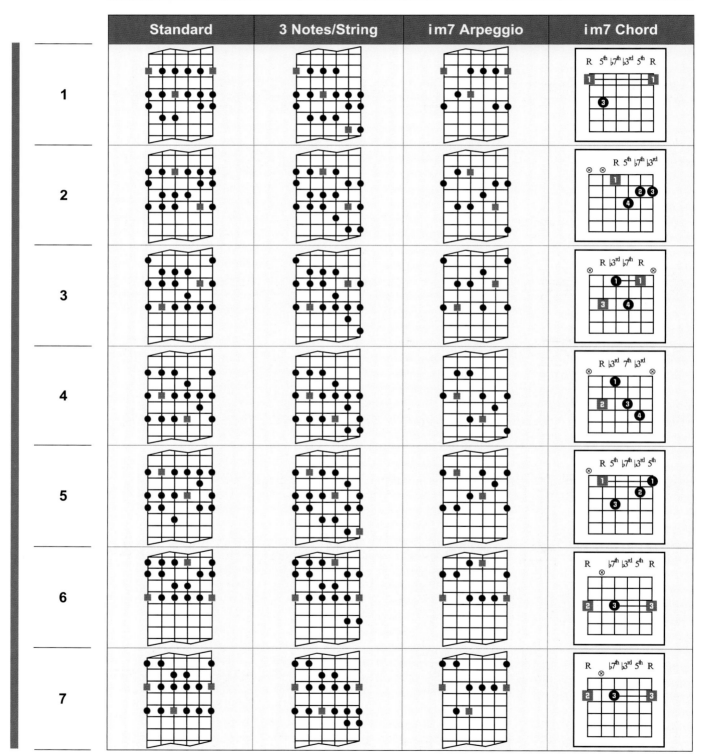

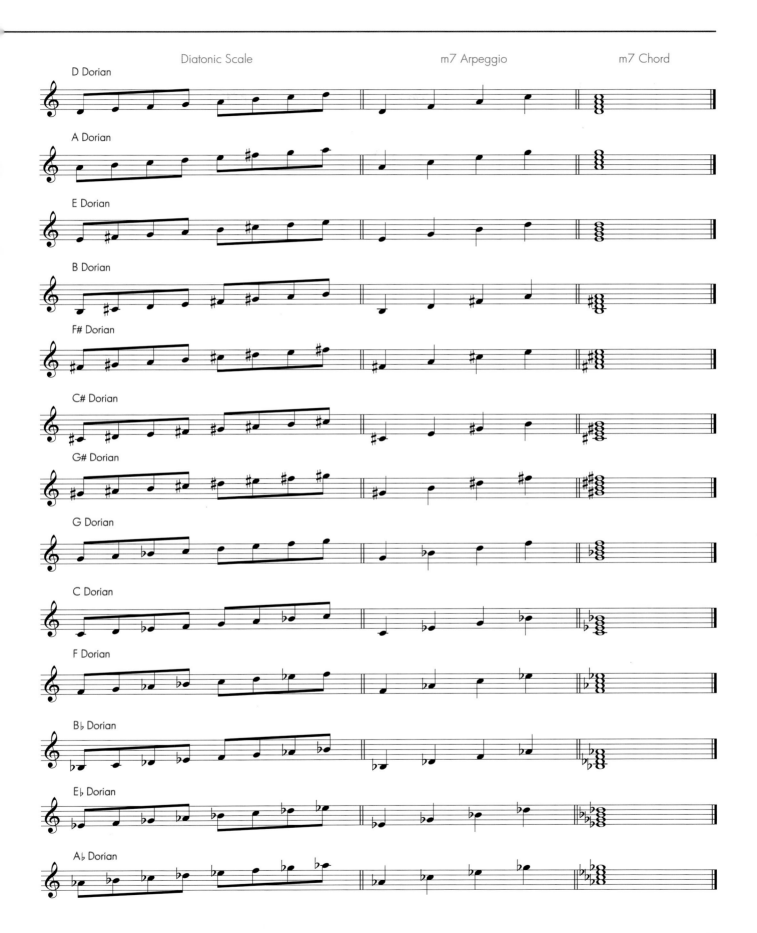

Third Mode of Major Scale: Phrygian Mode

The Phrygian Scale

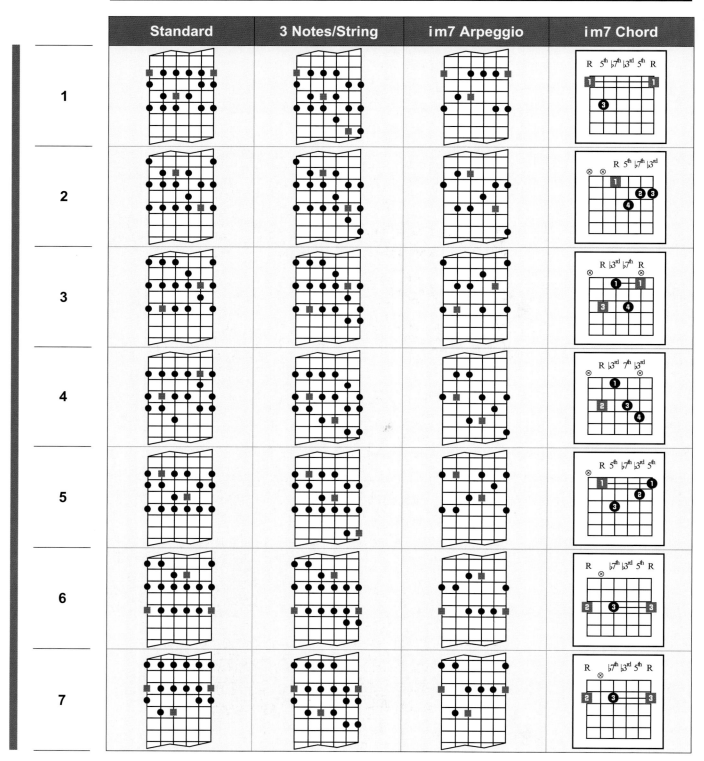

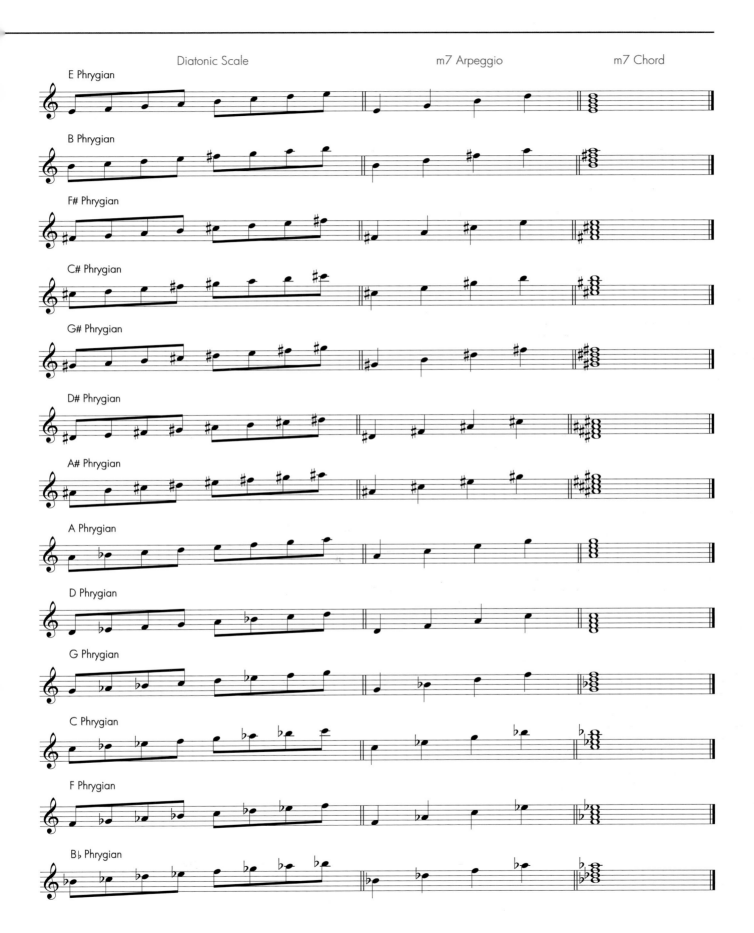

Fourth Mode of Major Scale: Lydian Mode

The Lydian Scale

	W	W	W	H	W	W	H
Scale Formula	1	2	3	#4	5	6	7	8
Harmonized Scale	Imaj7	II7	iiim7	#ivm7(♭5)	Vmaj7	vim7	viim7	Imaj7

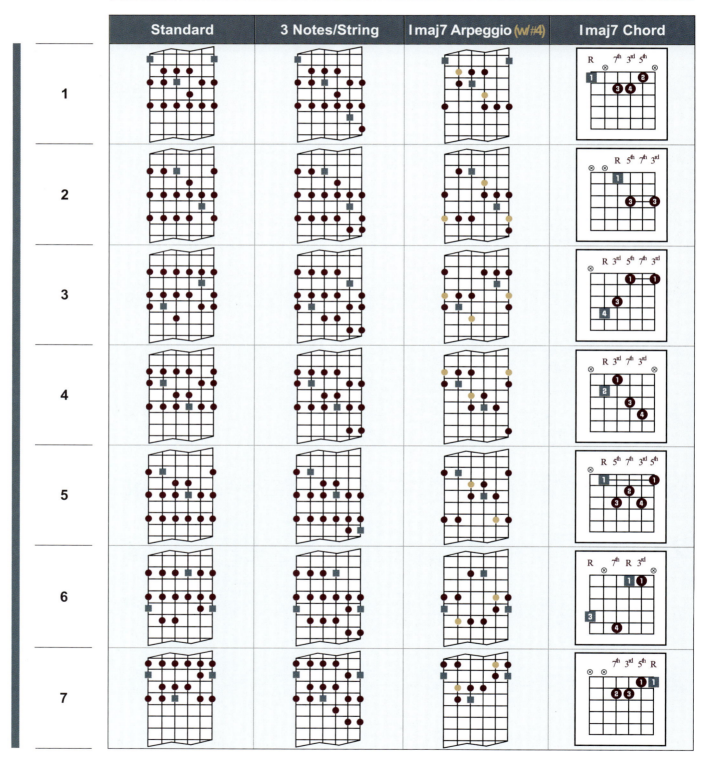

(The #4 is not part of the maj7 arpeggio, but is added for color.)

Fifth Mode of Major Scale: Mixolydian Mode

The Mixolydian Scale

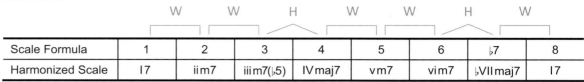
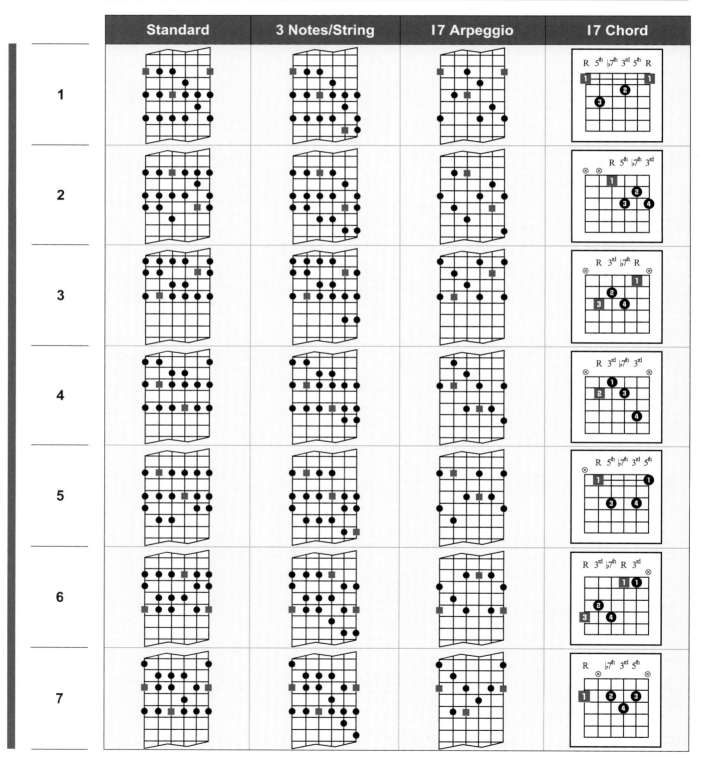

Sixth Mode of Major Scale: Aeolian Mode
The Natural Minor Scale*

	W	H	W	W	H	W	W
Scale Formula	1	2	♭3	4	5	♭6	♭7	8
Harmonized Scale	im7	iim7(♭5)	♭IIImaj7	ivm7	vm7	♭VImaj7	♭VII7	im7

	Standard	3 Notes/String	im7 Arpeggio	im7 Chord
1				
2				
3				
4				
5				
6				
7				

* aka The Pure Minor Scale

Seventh Mode of Major Scale: Locrian Mode
The Locrian Scale

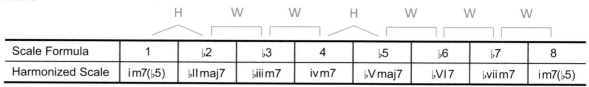

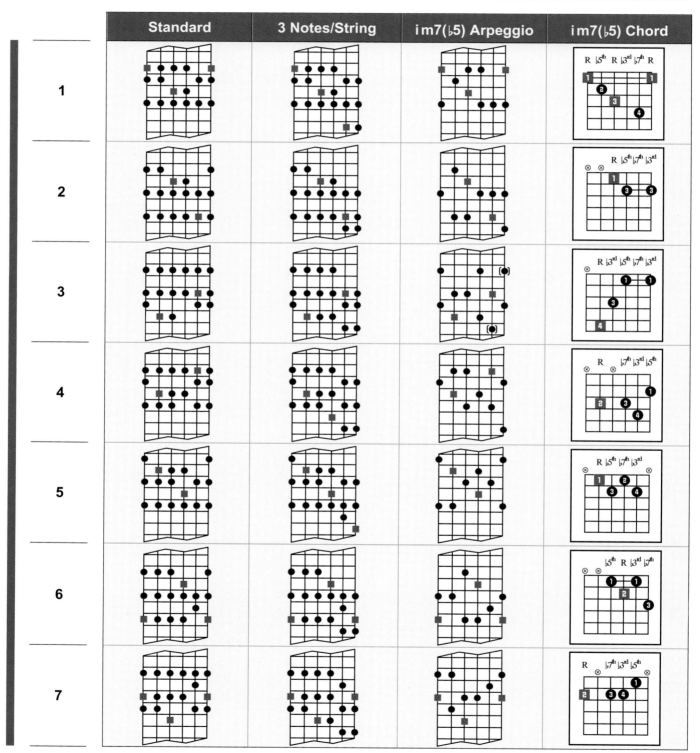

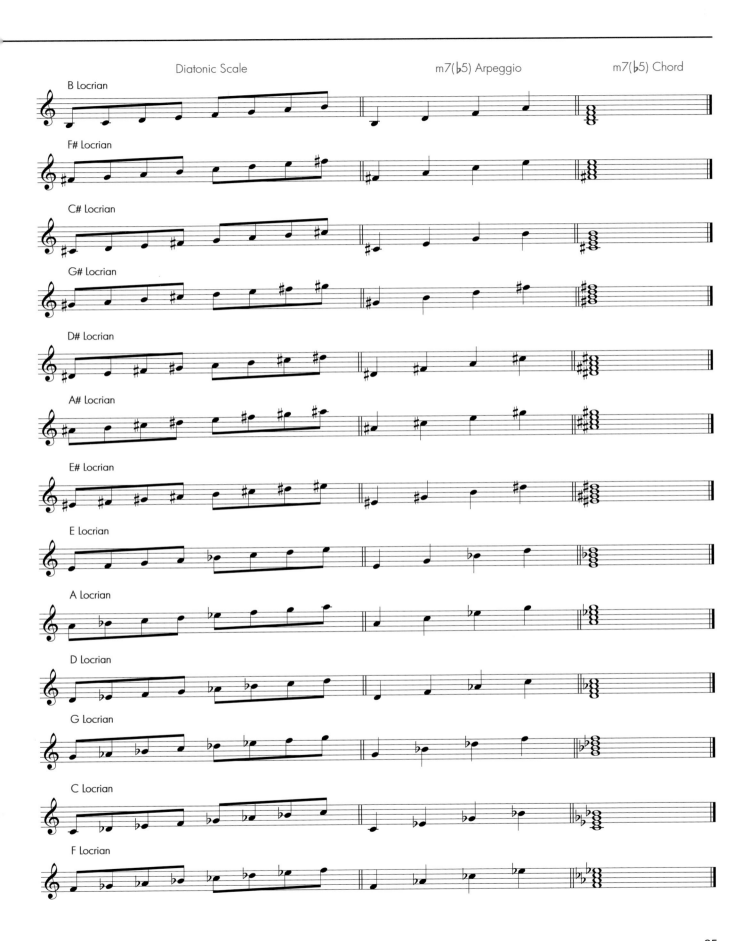

First Mode of Harmonic Minor Scale
The Harmonic Minor Scale

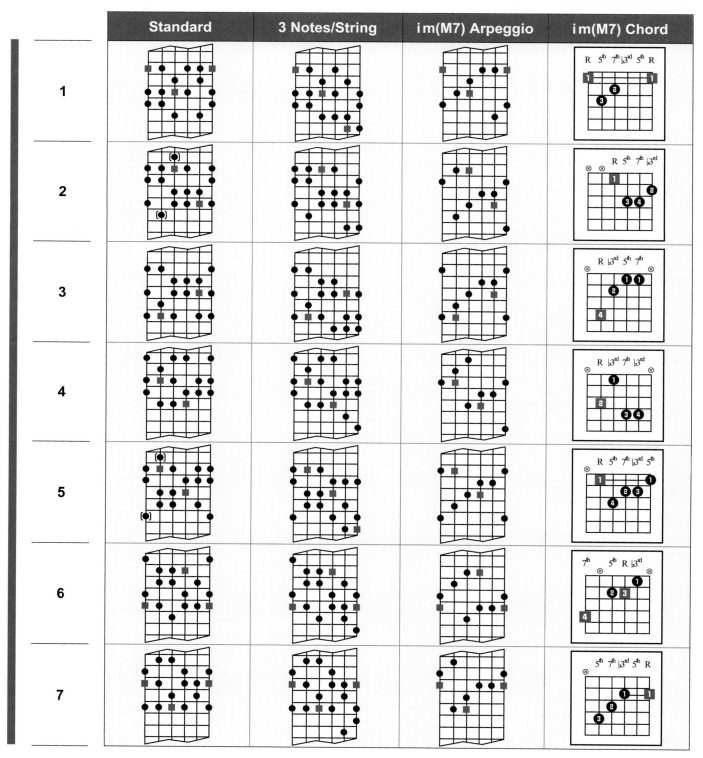

Second Mode of Harmonic Minor Scale

The Locrian ♮6 Scale

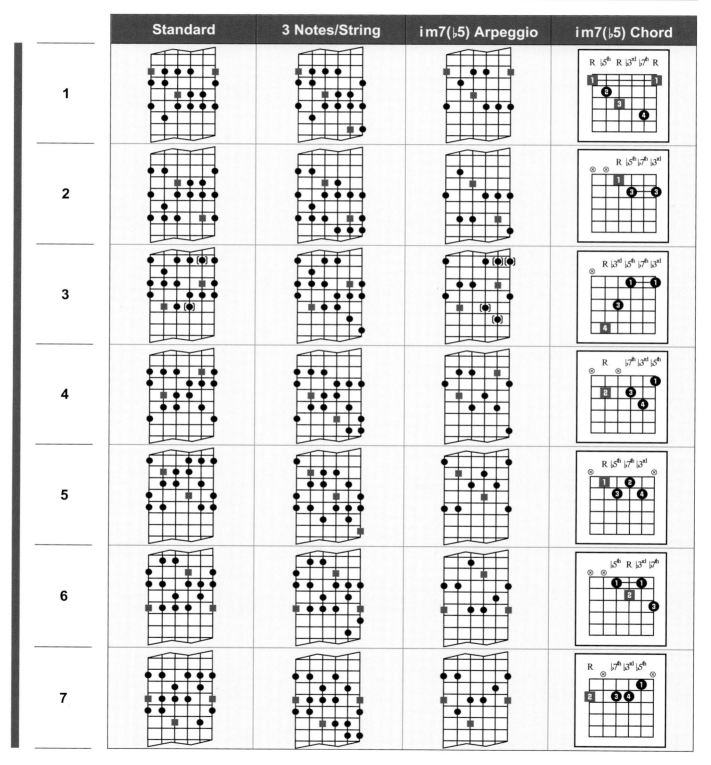

Third Mode of Harmonic Minor Scale
The Ionian #5 Scale

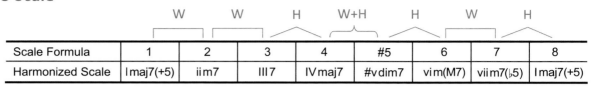

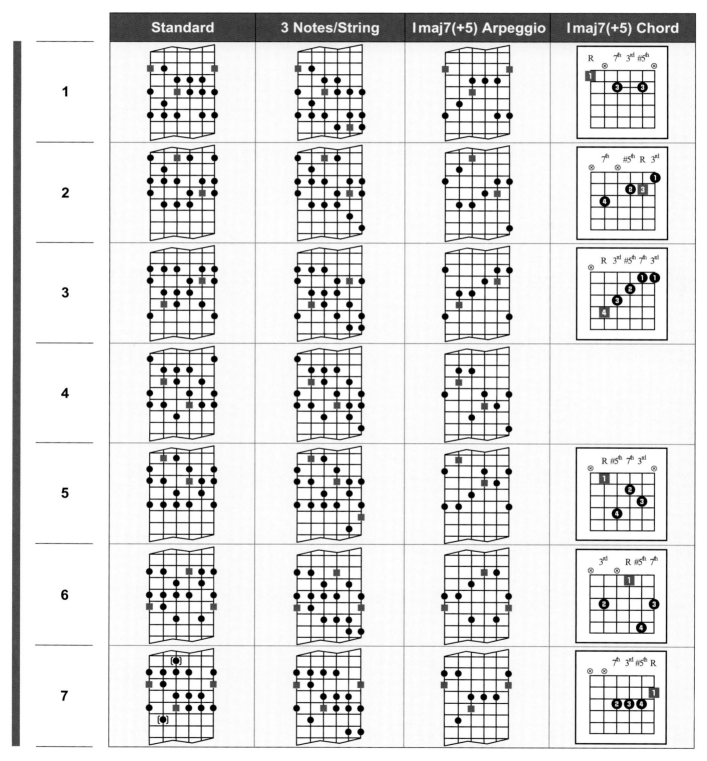

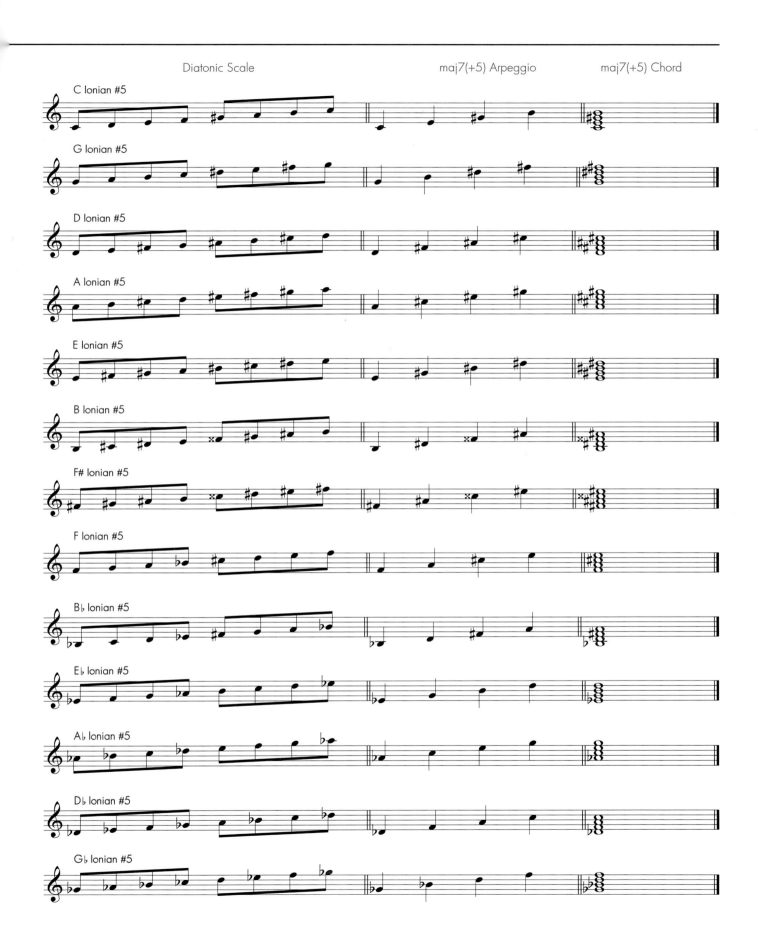

Fourth Mode of Harmonic Minor Scale
The Dorian #4 Scale

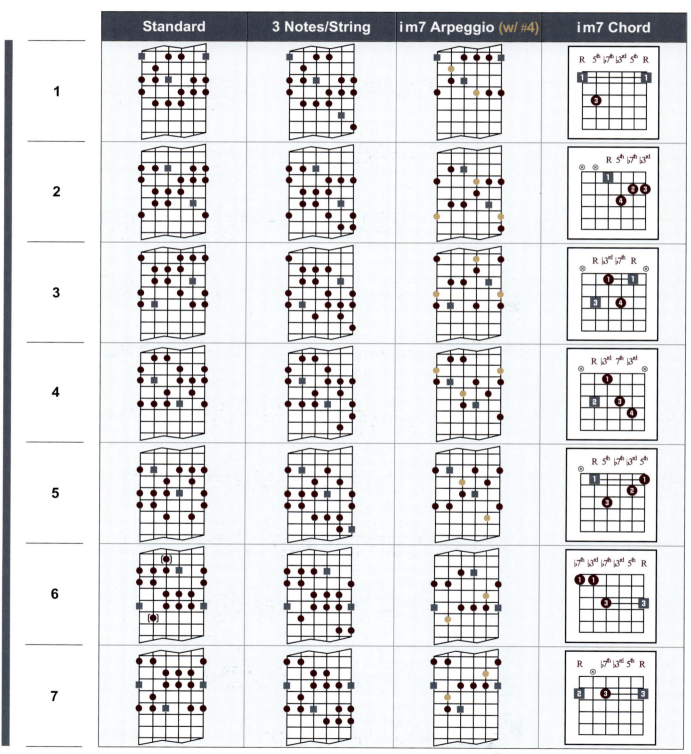

(The #4 is not part of the m7 arpeggio, but is added for color.)

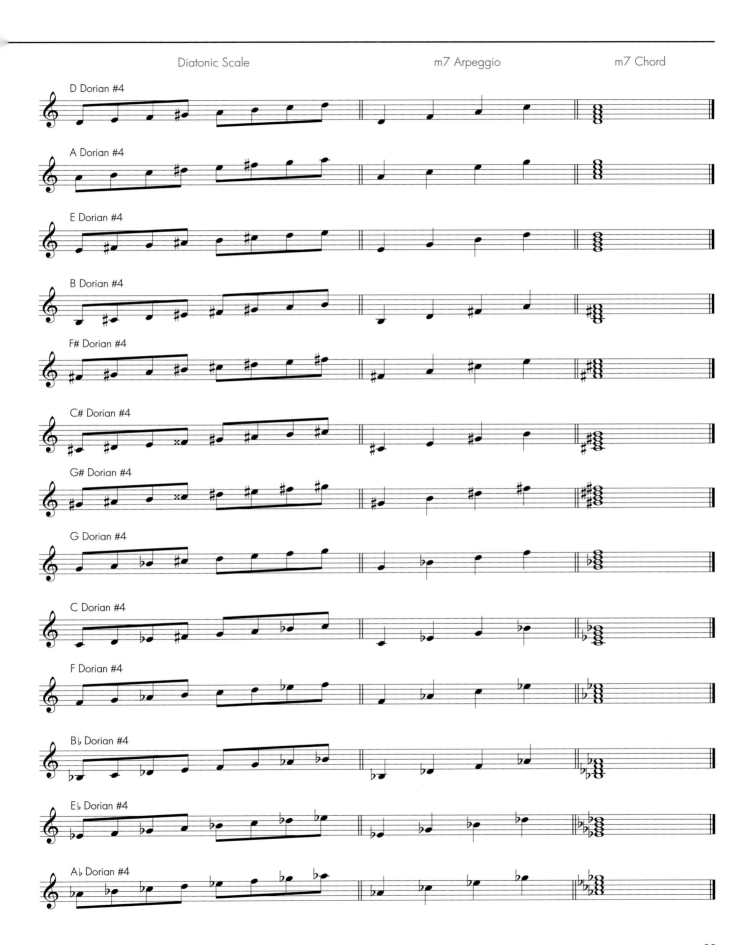

Fifth Mode of Harmonic Minor Scale

The Phrygian Dominant Scale*

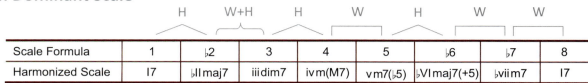

Scale Formula	1	♭2	3	4	5	♭6	♭7	8
Harmonized Scale	I7	♭IImaj7	iiidim7	ivm(M7)	vm7(♭5)	♭VImaj7(+5)	♭viim7	I7

Intervals above: H, W+H, H, W, H, W, W

*aka The Phrygian Major Scale

(The ♭2 is not part of the dom7 arpeggio, but is added for color.)

Columns: Standard | 3 Notes/String | I7 Arpeggio (w/ ♭2) | I7 Chord

Rows 1–7 show fretboard diagrams for each position.

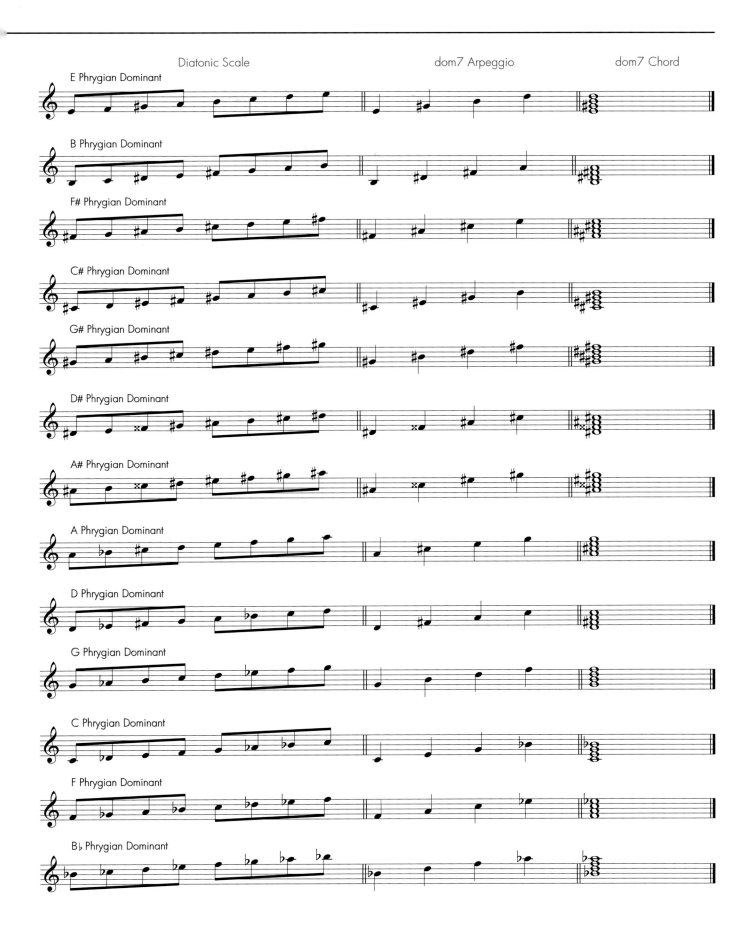

Sixth Mode of Harmonic Minor Scale
The Lydian #2 Scale

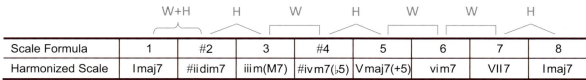

Scale Formula	1	#2	3	#4	5	6	7	8
Harmonized Scale	Imaj7	#iidim7	iiim(M7)	#ivm7(♭5)	Vmaj7(+5)	vim7	VII7	Imaj7

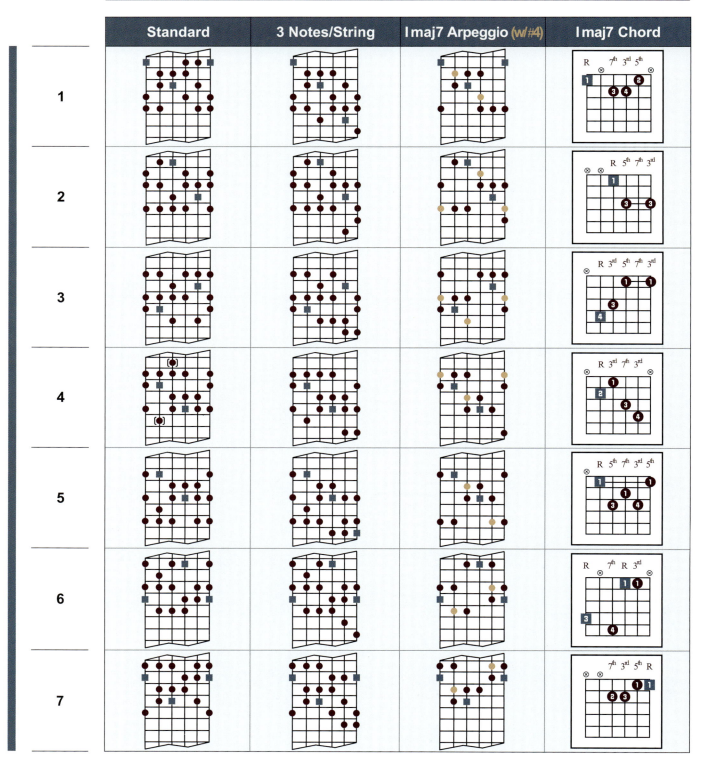

(The #4 is not part of the maj7 arpeggio, but is added for color.)

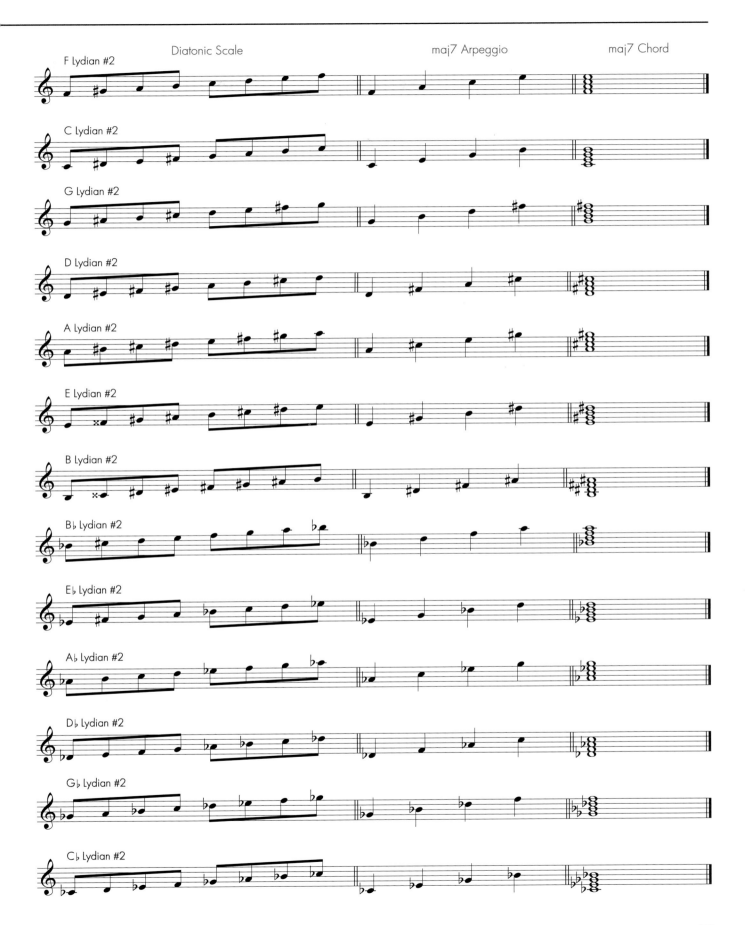

Seventh Mode of Harmonic Minor Scale

The Superlocrian ♭7 Scale

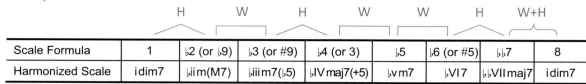

		H	W	H	W	W	H	W+H
Scale Formula	1	♭2 (or ♭9)	♭3 (or #9)	♭4 (or 3)	♭5	♭6 (or #5)	♭♭7	8
Harmonized Scale	idim7	♭iim(M7)	♭iiim7(♭5)	♭IVmaj7(+5)	♭vm7	♭VI7	♭♭VIImaj7	idim7

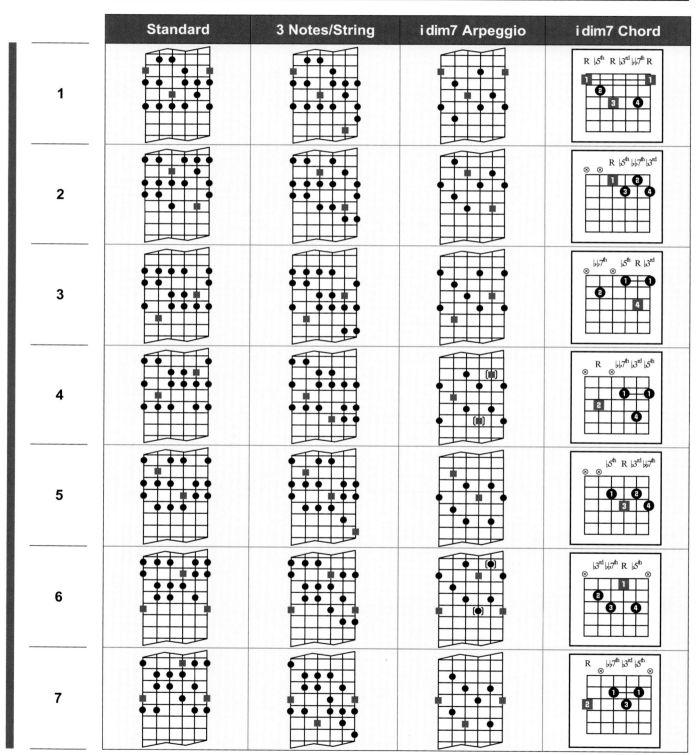

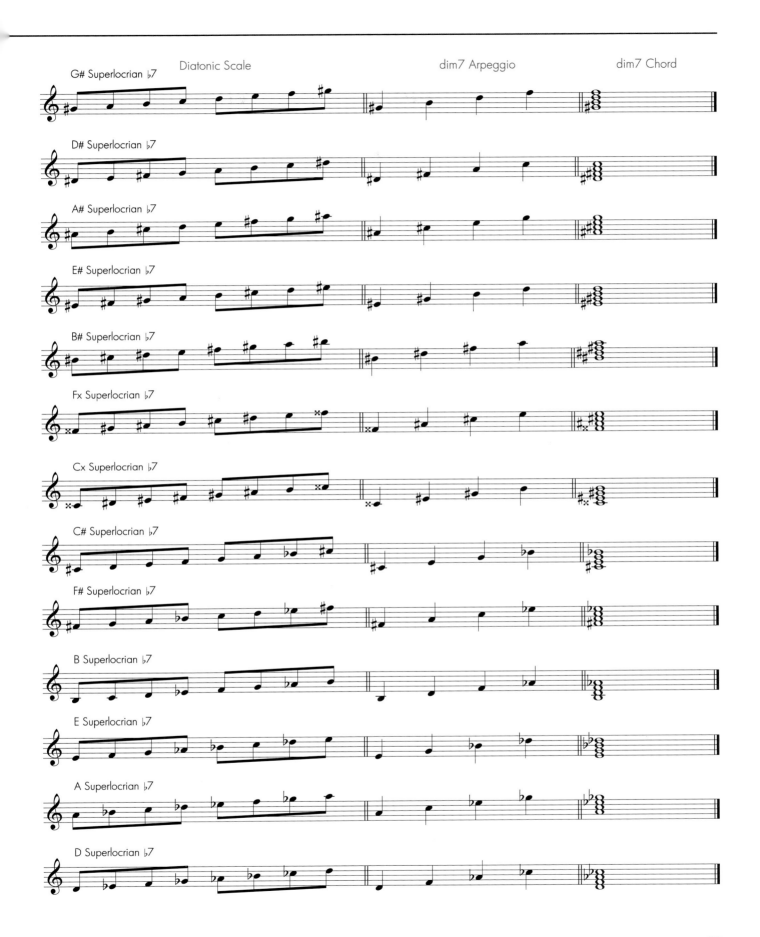

First Mode of Melodic Minor Scale

The Melodic Minor Scale

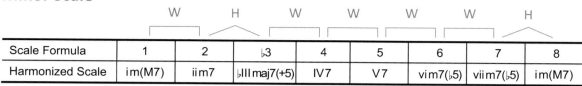

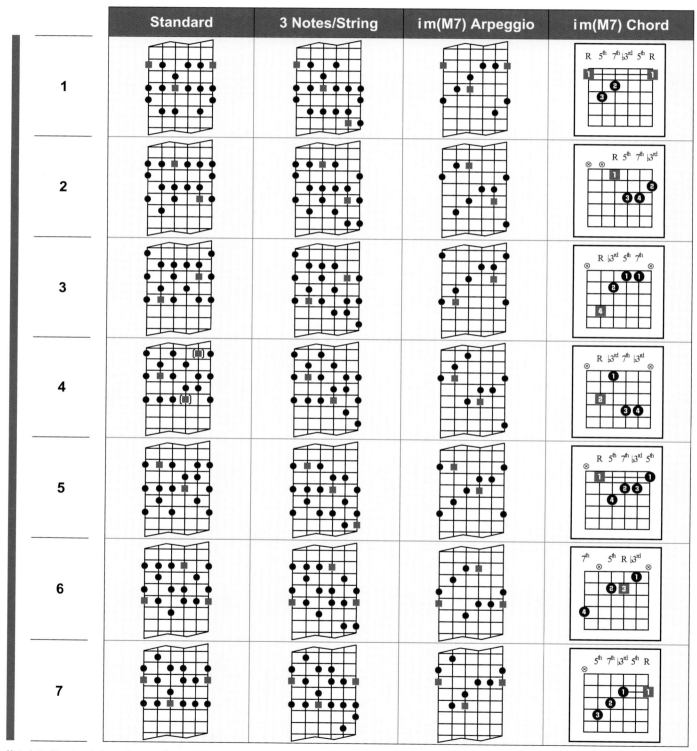

Note: In traditional music theory, the <u>ascending</u> melodic scale is played as shown above, but the <u>descending</u> melodic minor scale is played as the natural minor scale. The modern trend is to play the scale shown above for <u>both ascending and descending</u> movement – and that scale is sometimes called the "jazz melodic minor scale" or simply the "jazz minor scale."

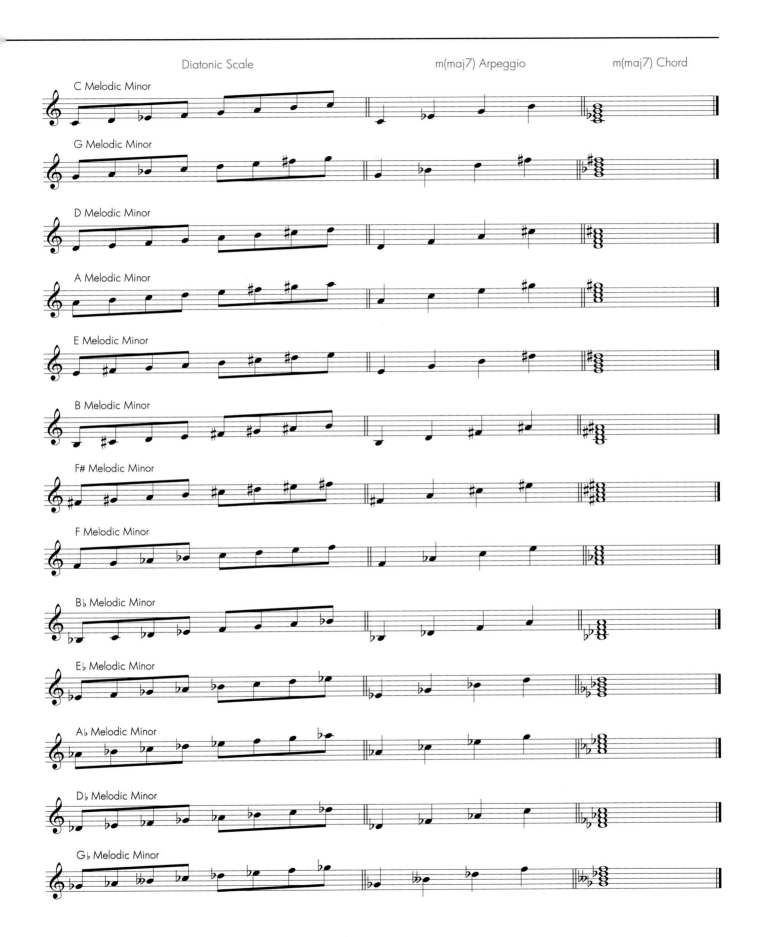

Second Mode of Melodic Minor Scale

The Dorian ♭2 Scale

	H	W	W	W	W	H	W
Scale Formula	1	♭2	♭3	4	5	6	♭7	8
Harmonized Scale	im7	♭IImaj7(+5)	♭III7	IV7	vm7(♭5)	vim7(♭5)	♭viim(M7)	im7

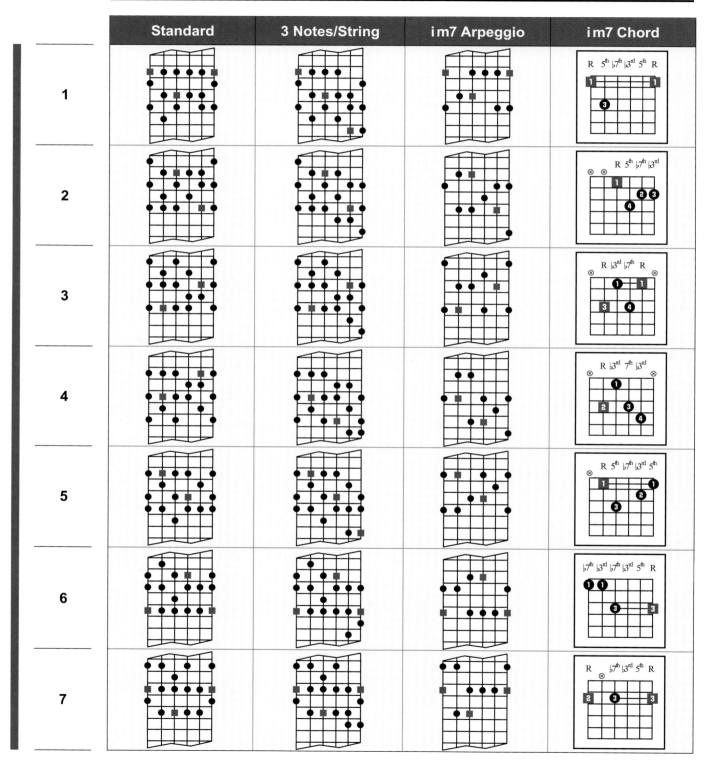

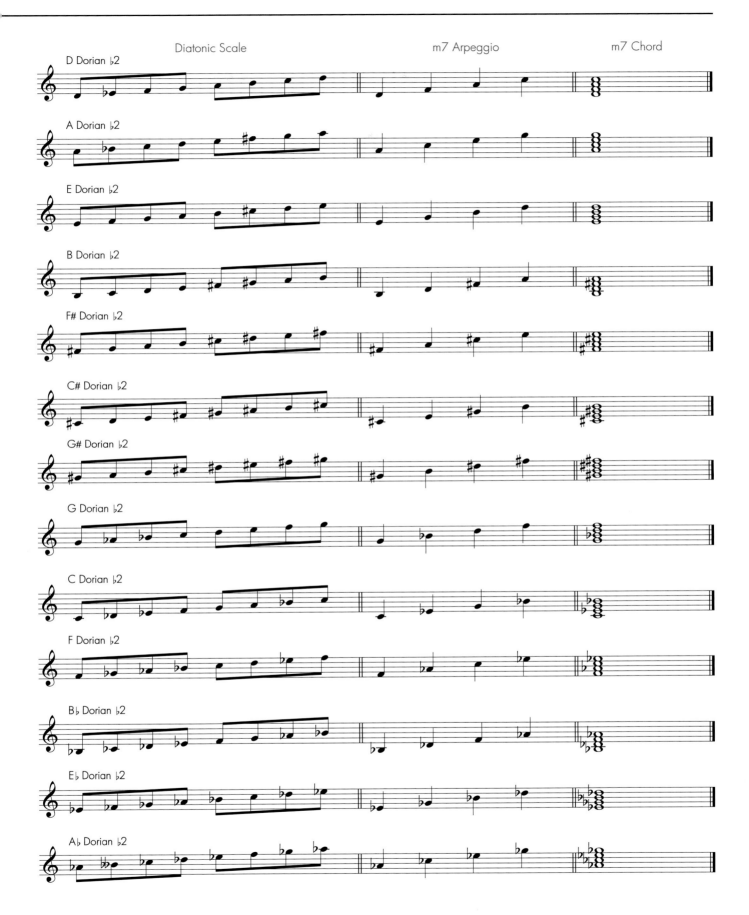

Third Mode of Melodic Minor Scale
The Lydian Augmented Scale

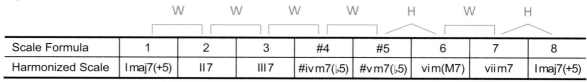

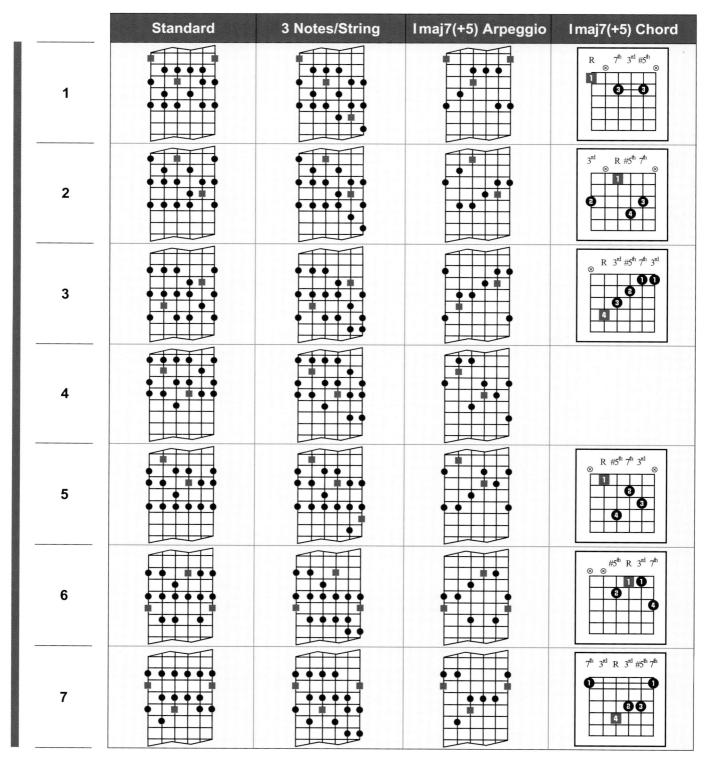

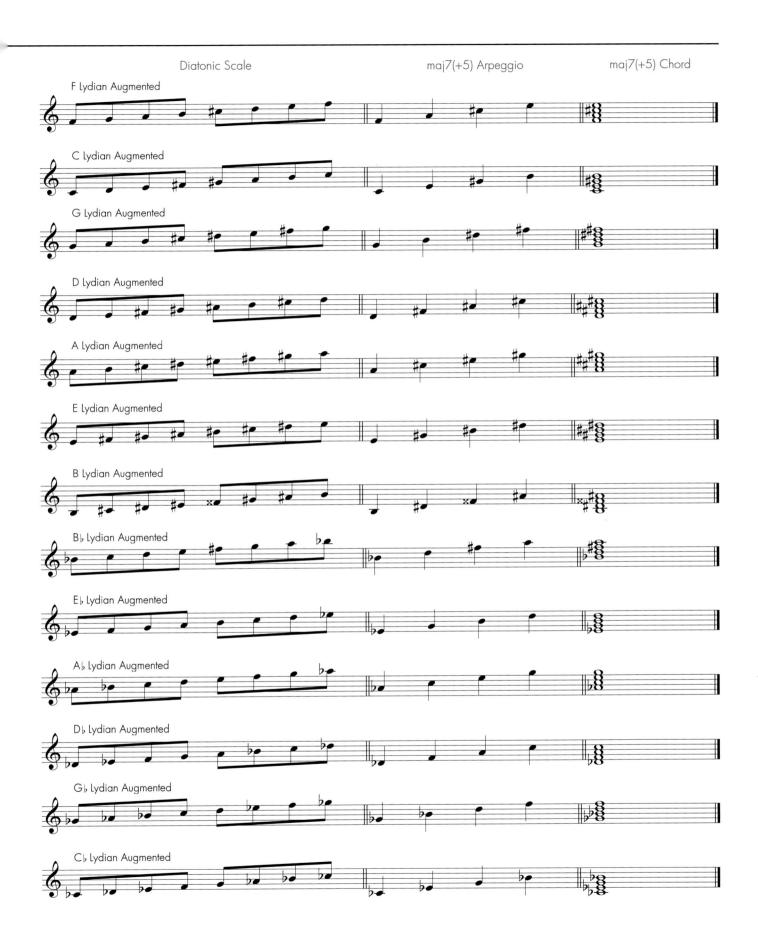

Fourth Mode of Melodic Minor Scale

The Lydian ♭7 Scale

	W	W	W	H	W	H	W
Scale Formula	1	2	3	#4	5	6	♭7	8
Harmonized Scale	I7	II7	iiim7(♭5)	#ivm7(♭5)	vm(M7)	vim7	♭VIImaj7(+5)	I7

	Standard	3 Notes/String	I7 Arpeggio (w/ #4)	I7(♭5) Chord*
1				
2				
3				
4				
5				
6				
7				

*Substitute for I7 Chord

(The #4 is not part of the dom7 arpeggio, but is added for color.)

Fifth Mode of Melodic Minor Scale

The Mixolydian ♭6 Scale

	W	W	H	W	H	W	W
Scale Formula	1	2	3	4	5	♭6	♭7	8
Harmonized Scale	I7	iim7(♭5)	iiim7(♭5)	ivm(M7)	vm7	♭VImaj7(+5)	♭VII7	I7

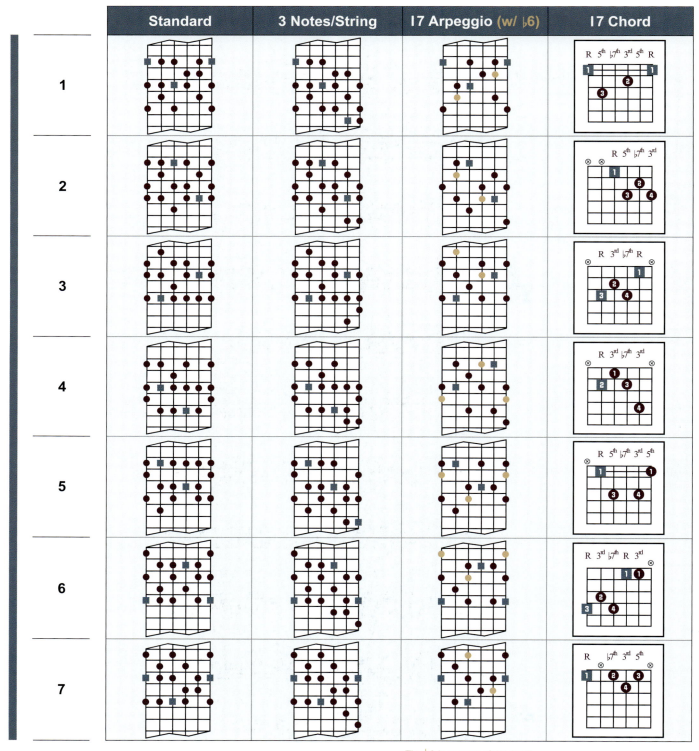

(The ♭6 is not part of the dom7 arpeggio, but is added for color.)

48 ©2009 Guy's Publishing Group, LLC

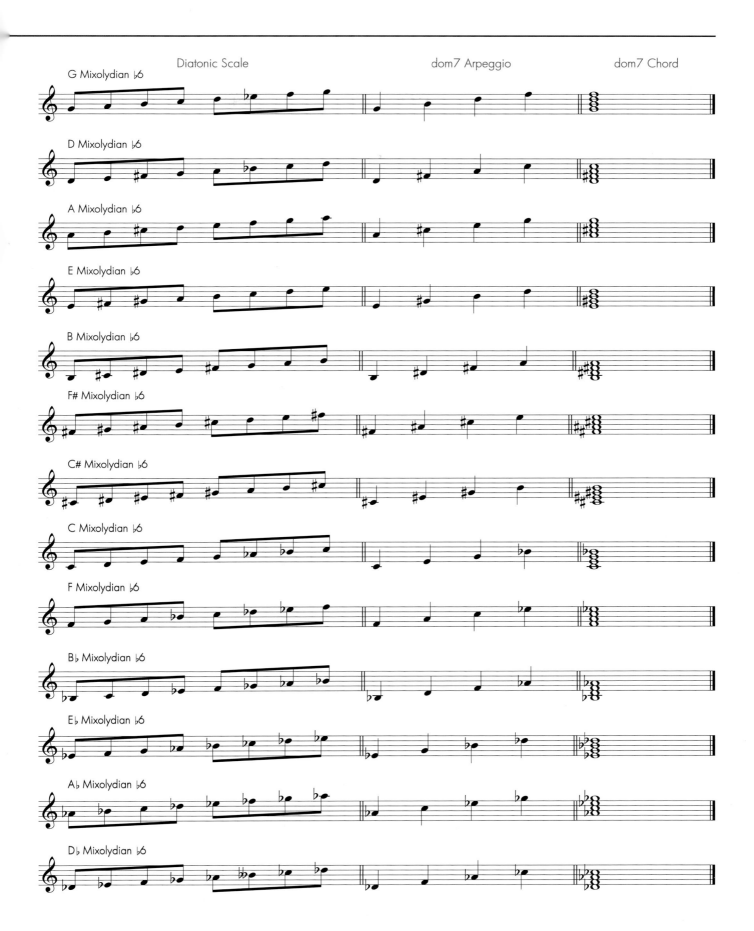

Sixth Mode of Melodic Minor Scale

The Locrian ♮2 Scale

Scale Formula	1	2	♭3	4	♭5	♭6	♭7	8
Harmonized Scale	im7(♭5)	iim7(♭5)	♭iiim(M7)	ivm7	♭Vmaj7(+5)	♭VI7	♭VII7	im7(♭5)

Intervals: W H W H W W W

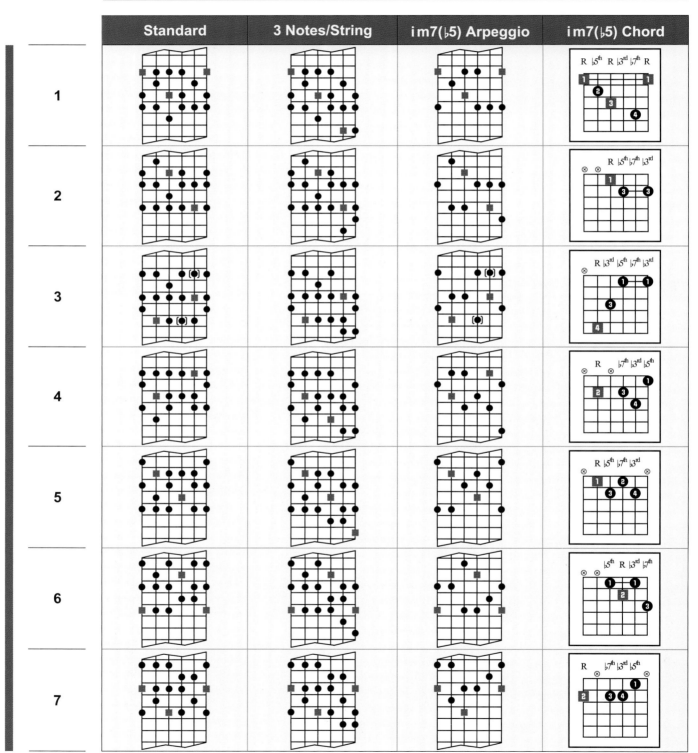

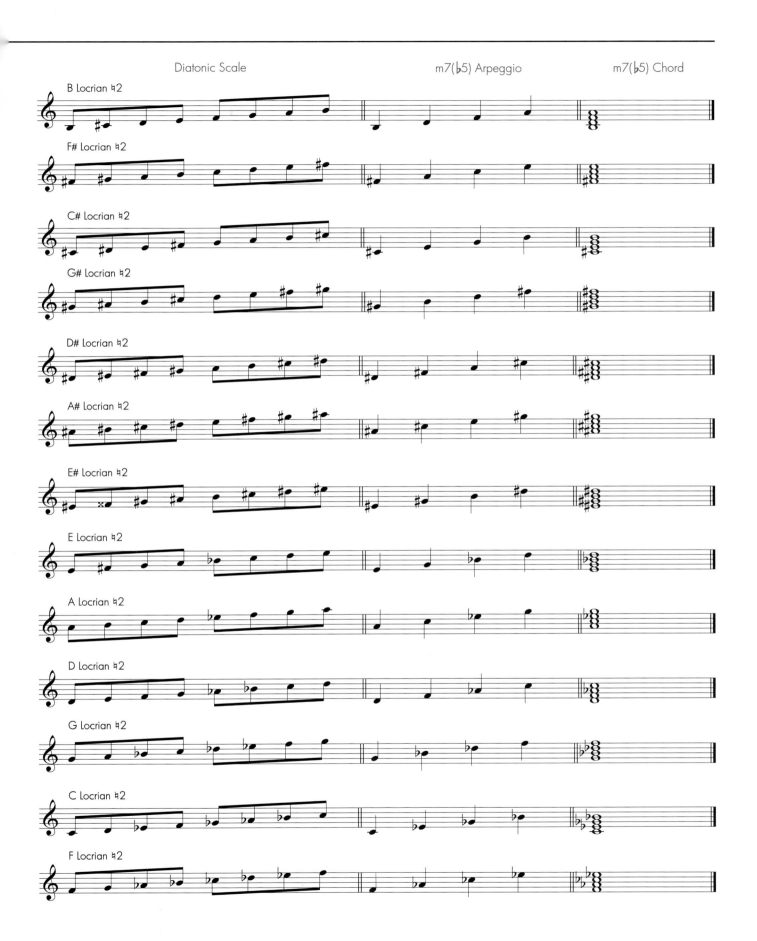

Seventh Mode of Melodic Minor Scale
The Altered Scale*

		H	W	H	W	W	W	W
Scale Formula	1	♭2 (or ♭9)	#2 (or #9)	3	♭5	#5	♭7	8
Harmonized Scale	im7(♭5)	♭iim(M7)	#iim7	IIImaj7(+5)	♭V7	#V7	♭viim7(♭5)	im7(♭5)

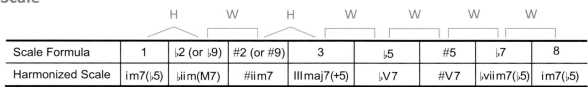

	Standard	3 Notes/String	17+5(#9) Arpeggio	17+5(#9) Chord
1				
2				
3				
4				
5				
6				
7				

*aka the Superlocrian Scale or the Diminished Whole Tone Scale

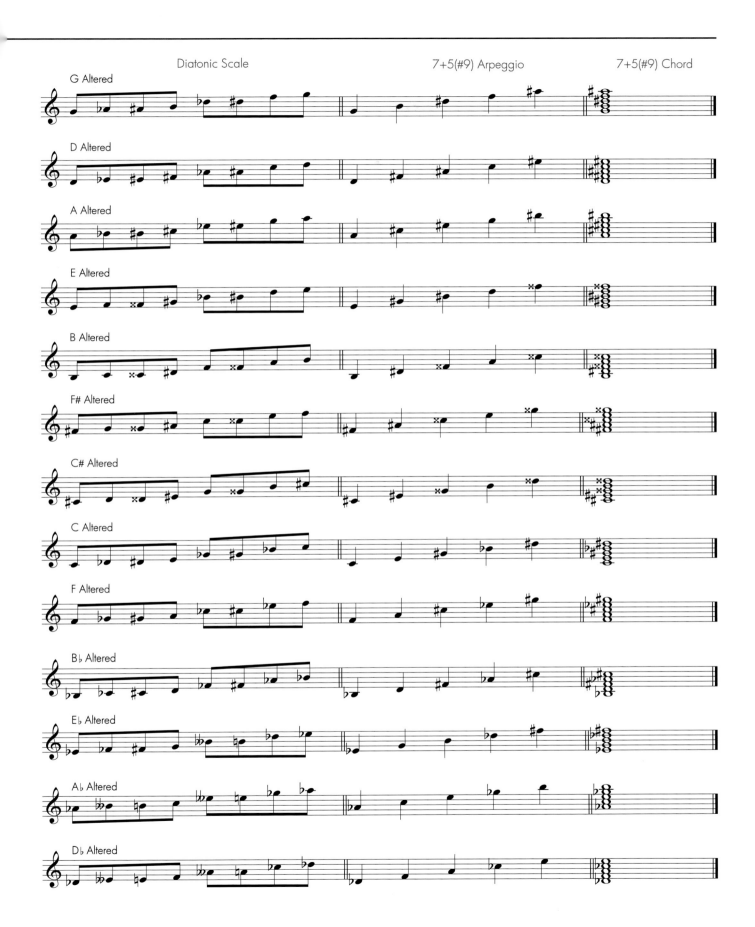

The Major Pentatonic Scale

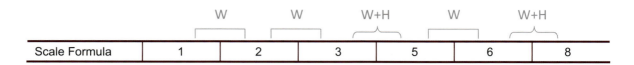
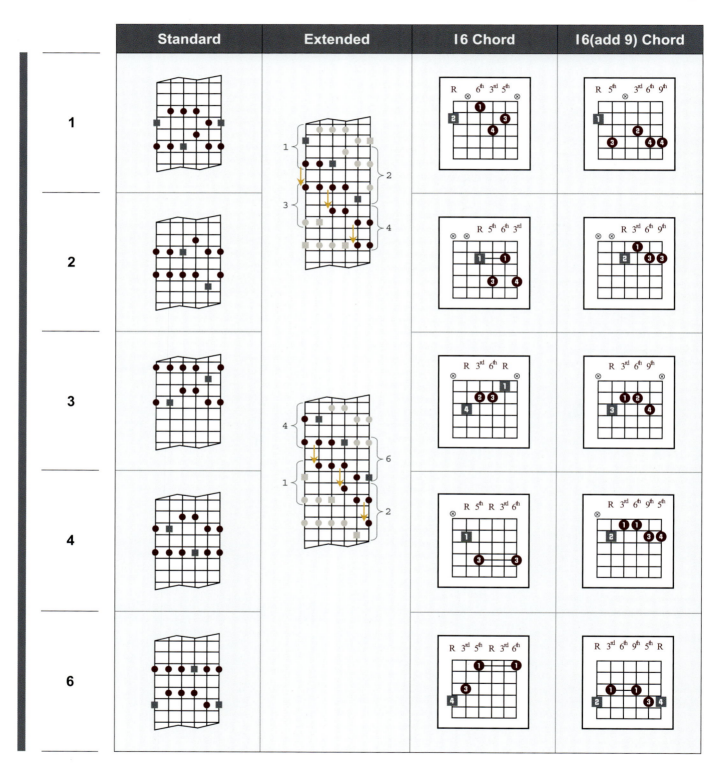

The Major Blues Scale

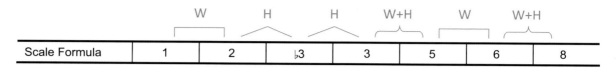
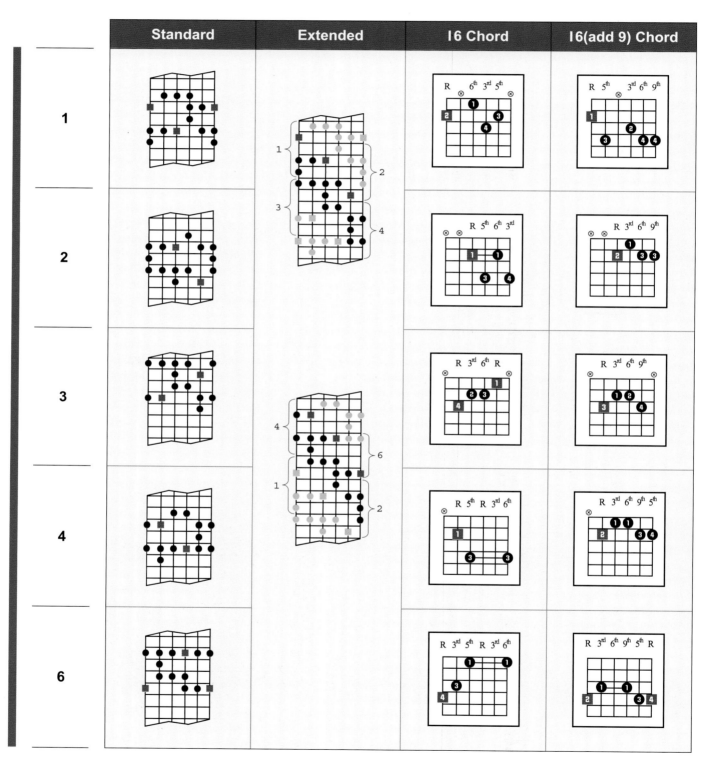

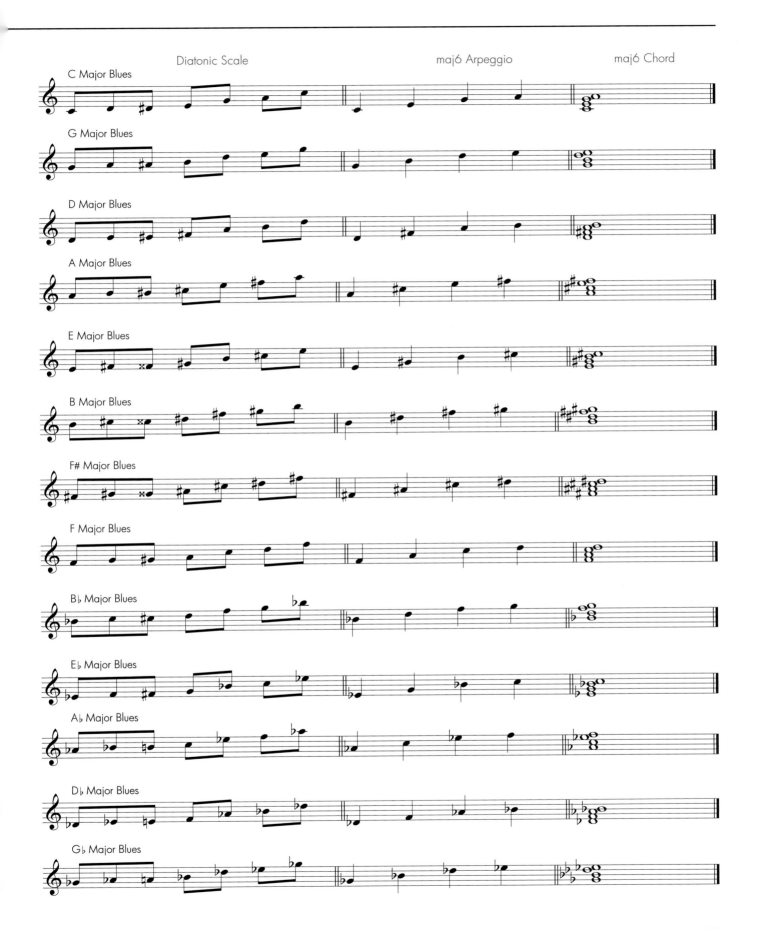

The Minor Pentatonic Scale

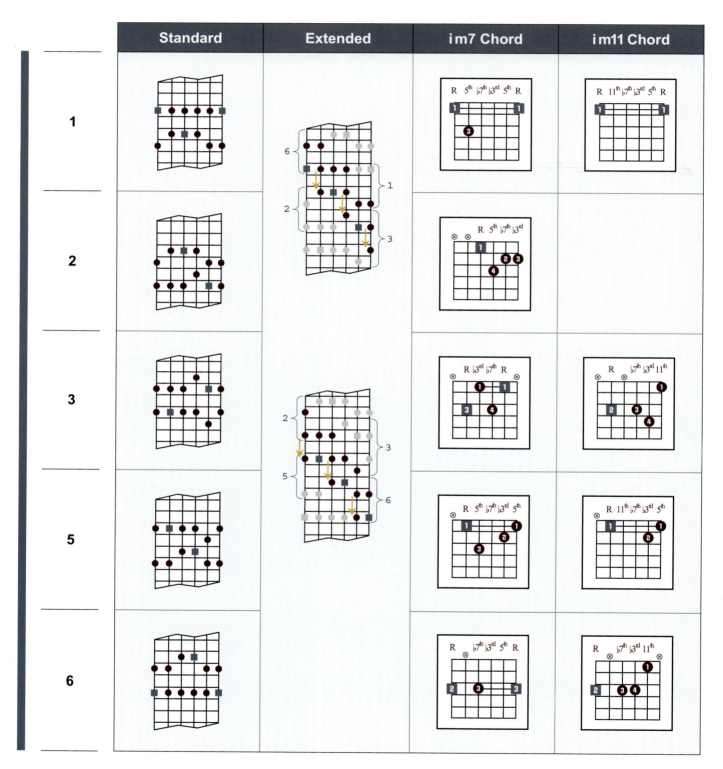

The Minor Blues Scale

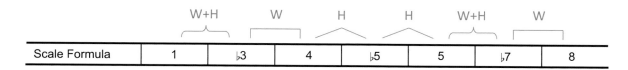
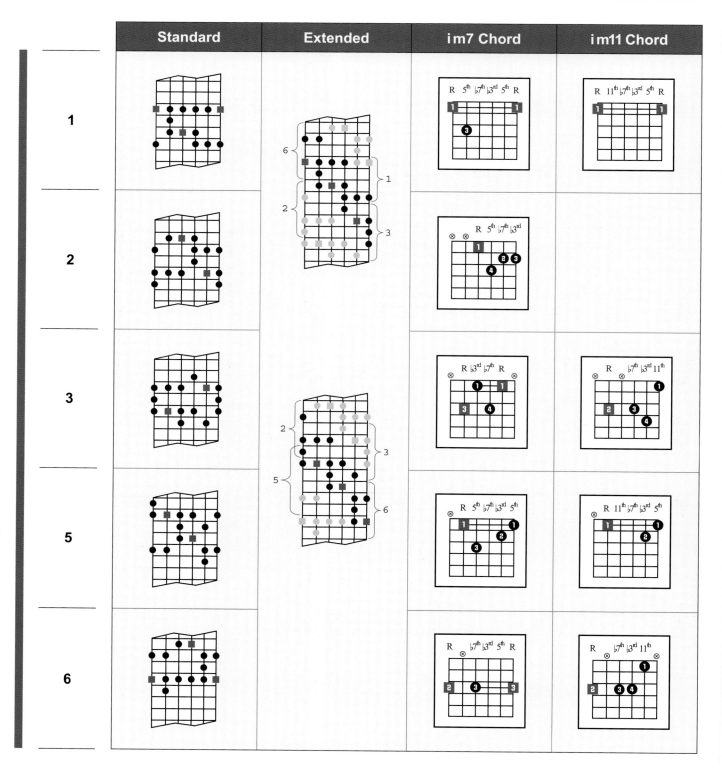

The Dominant Diminished Scale*

| | Scale Formula | 1 | ♭2 (or ♭9) | #2 (or #9) | 3 | #4 (or #11) | 5 | 6 (or 13) | ♭7 | 8 |

Interval pattern: H W H W H W H W

	Scale	I7 Arpeggio	I7 Chord
1			R 5th ♭7th 3rd 5th R
2			R 5th ♭7th 3rd
3			R 3rd ♭7th R
4			R 3rd ♭7th 3rd
5			R 5th ♭7th 3rd 5th
6			R 3rd ♭7th R 3rd
7			R ♭7th 3rd 5th

* aka The Half-Whole Diminished Scale

The Diminished Scale*

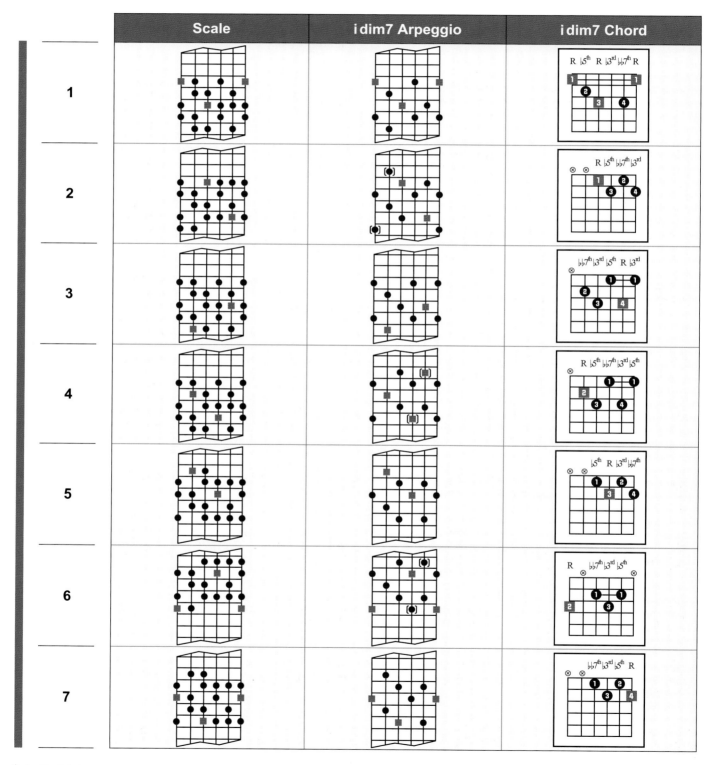

* aka The Whole-Half Diminished Scale

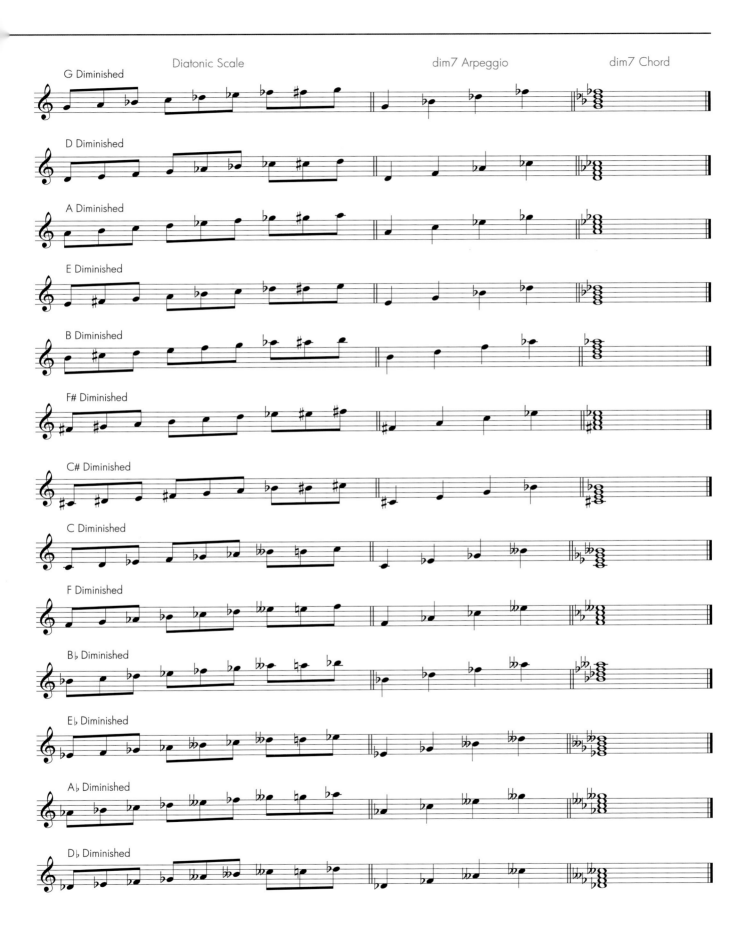

The Whole Tone Scale

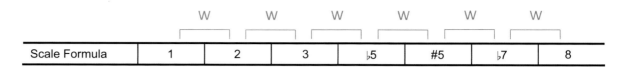

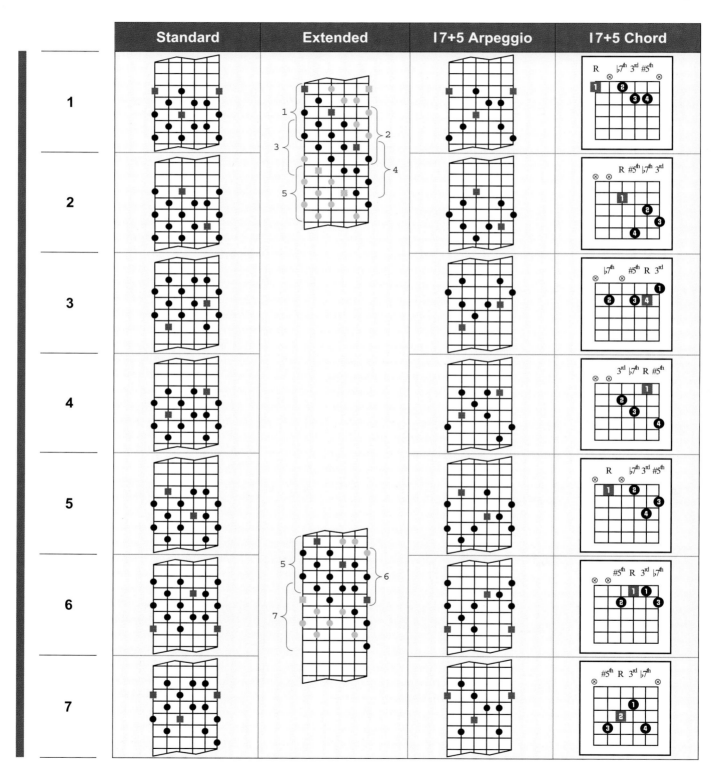

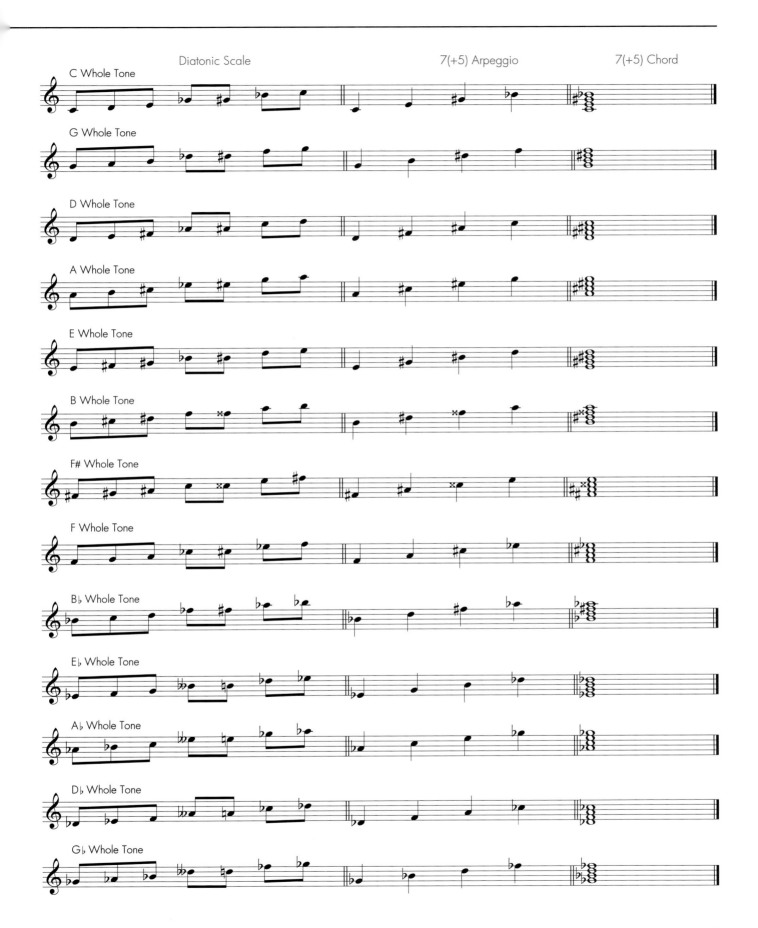

APPENDIX

Major Triad Study

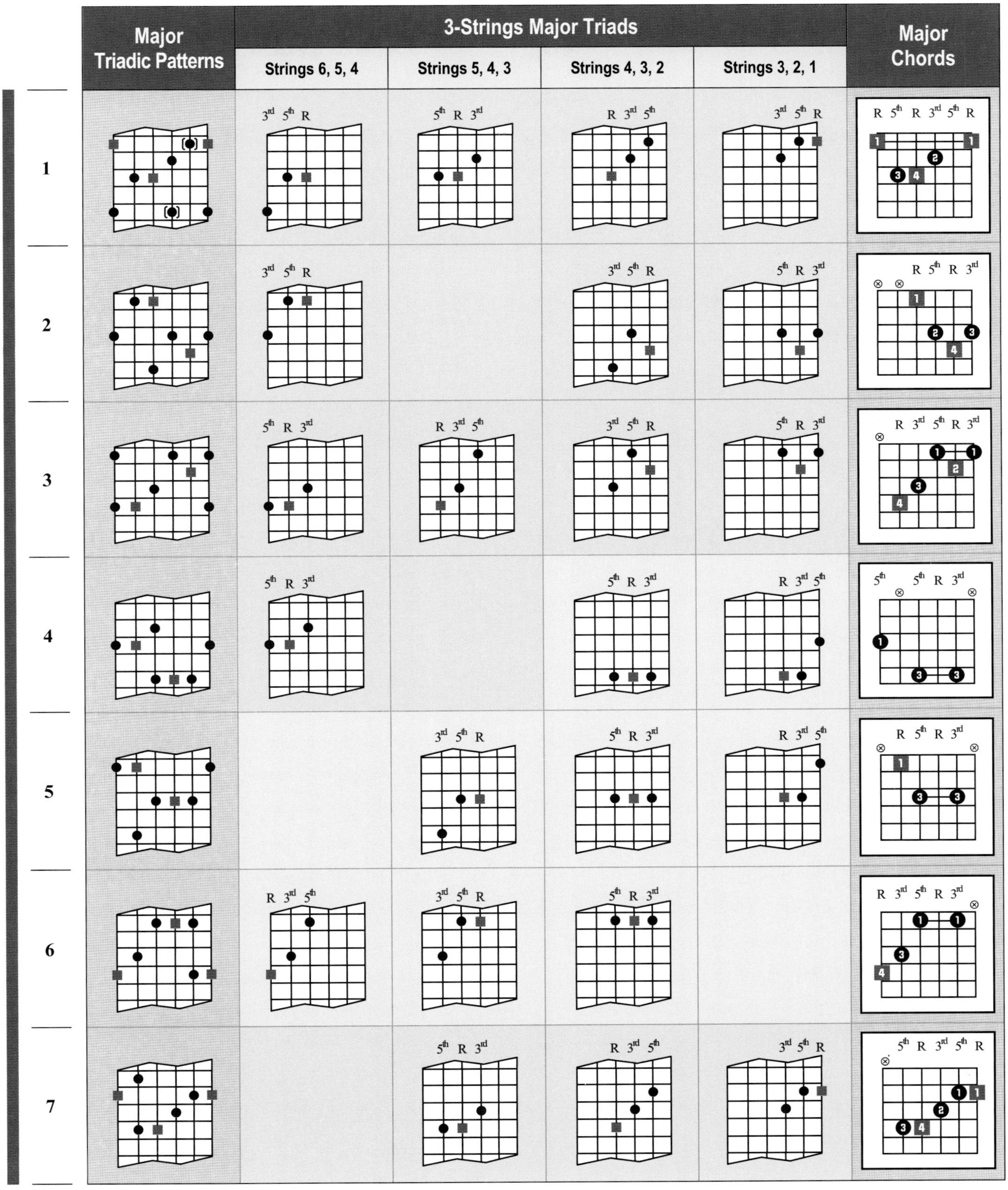

Minor Triad Study

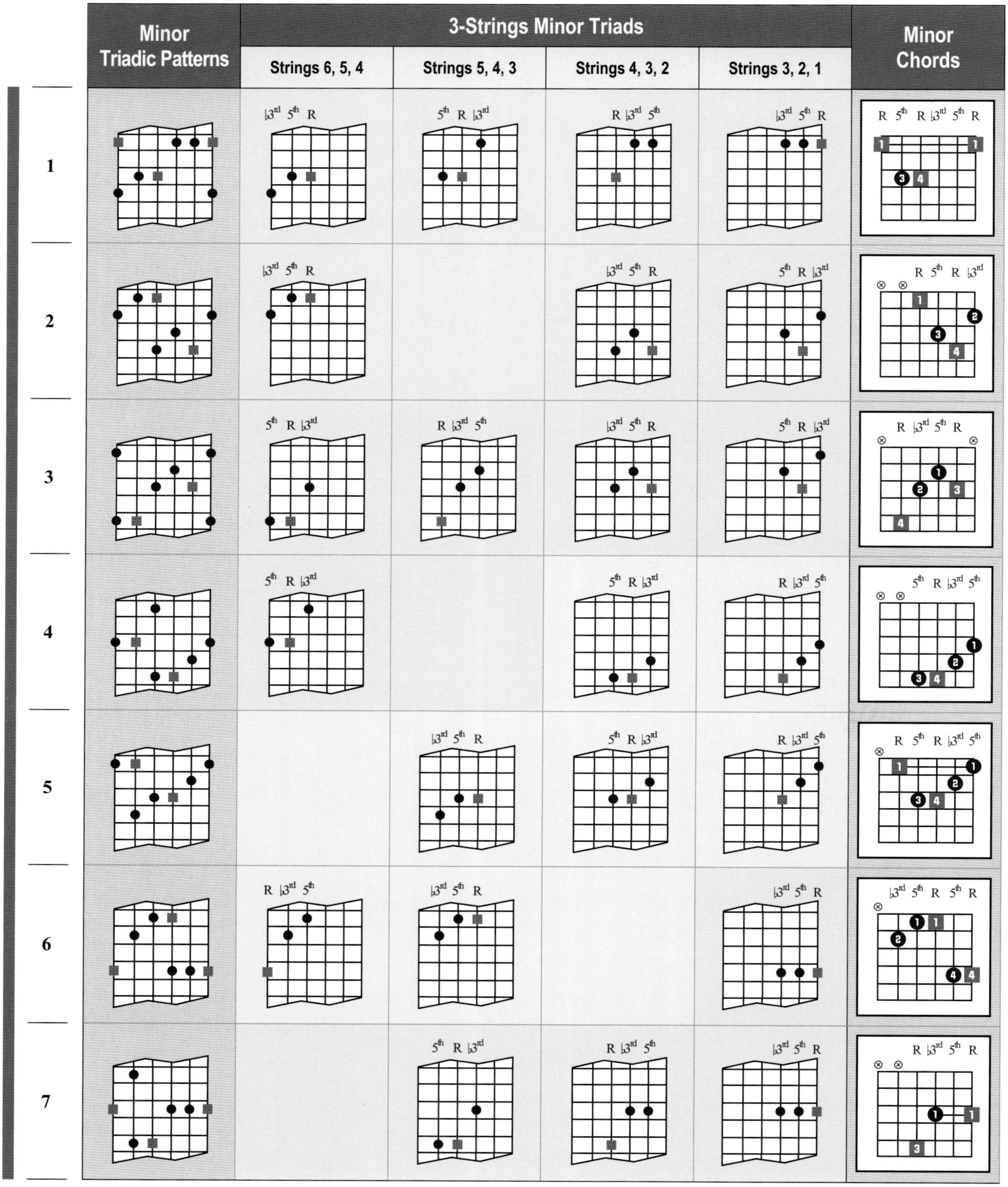

DIMINISHED TRIAD STUDY

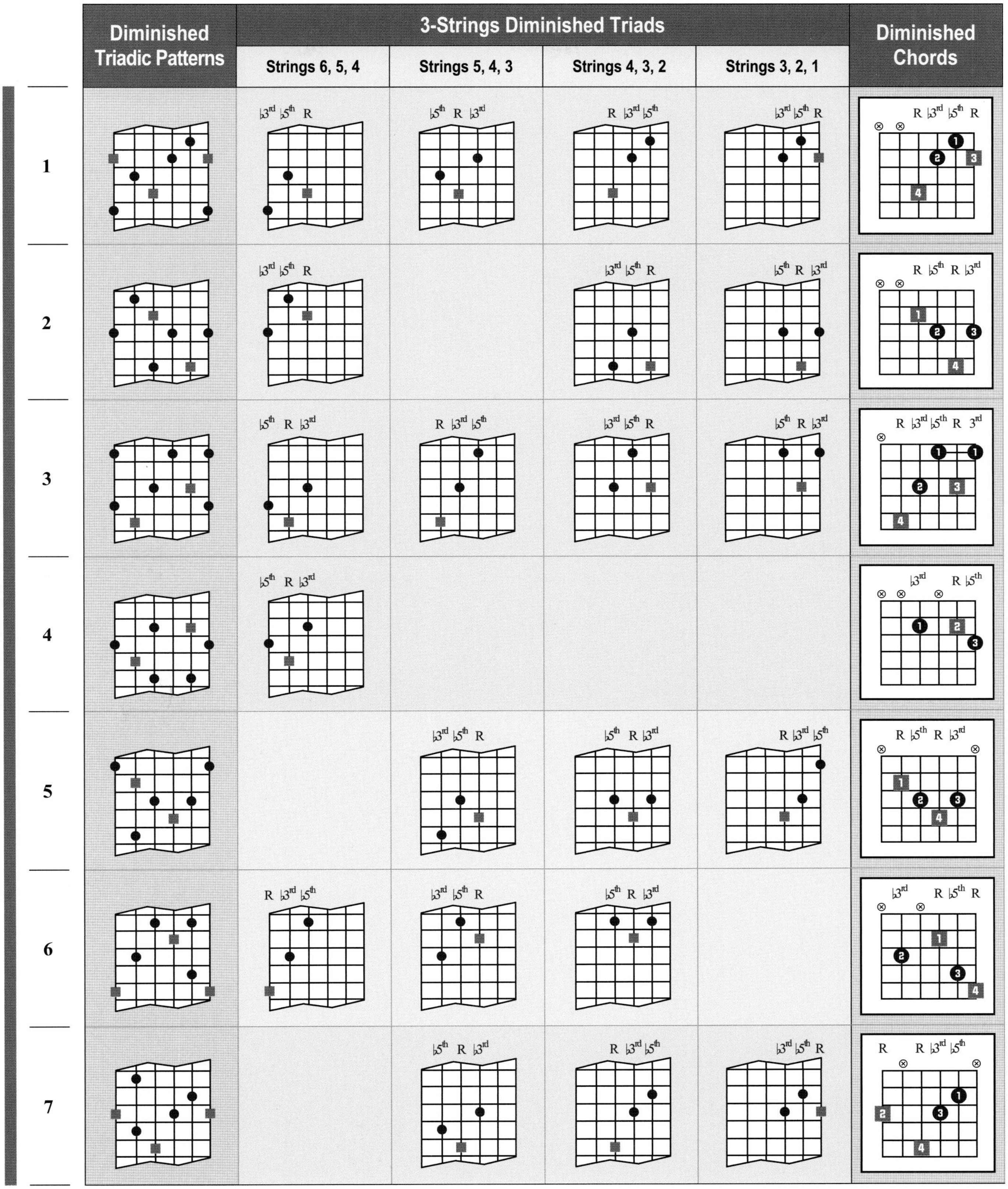

Augmented Triad Study

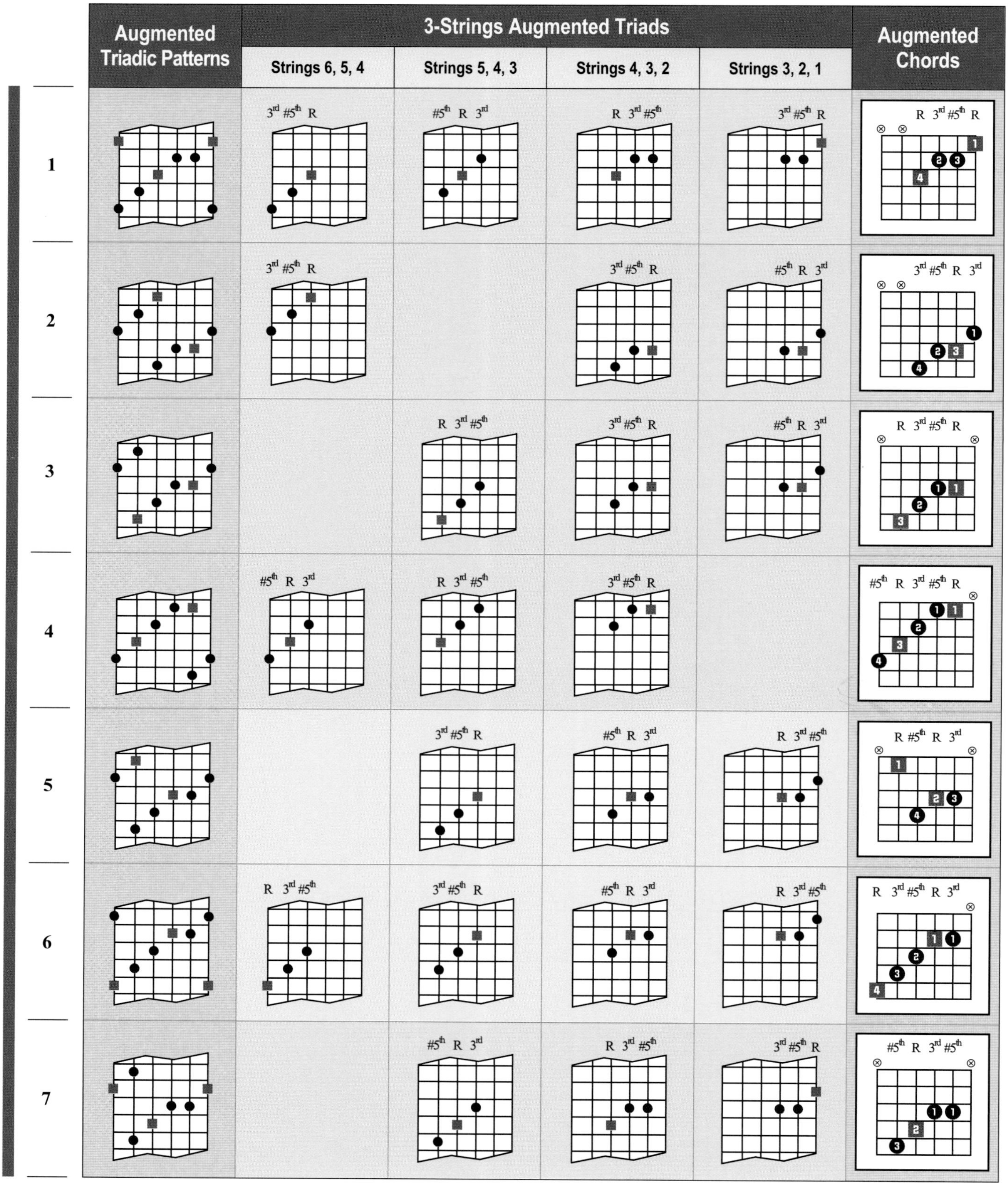

Sus2 Triad Study

	Sus2 Triadic Patterns	3-Strings Sus2 Triads				Sus2 Chords
		Strings 6, 5, 4	Strings 5, 4, 3	Strings 4, 3, 2	Strings 3, 2, 1	
1	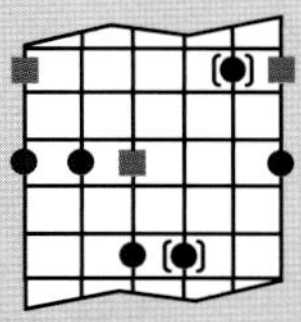	2nd 5th R 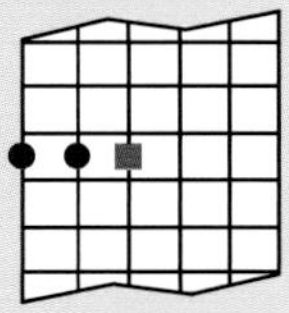				
2	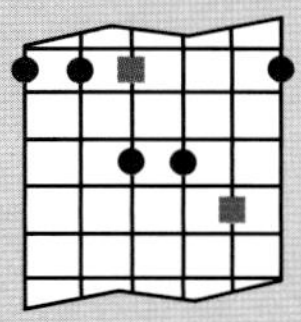	2nd 5th R 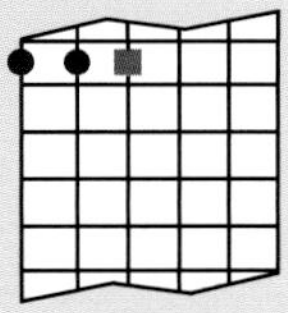		2nd 5th R 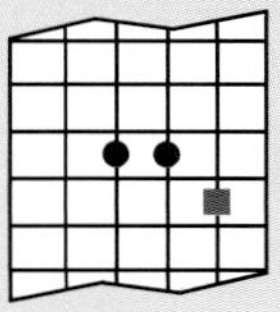	5th R 2nd 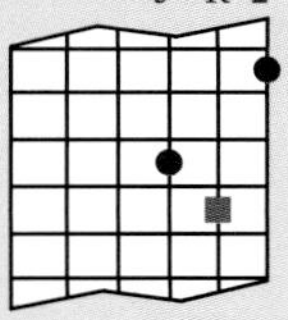	R 5th R 2nd 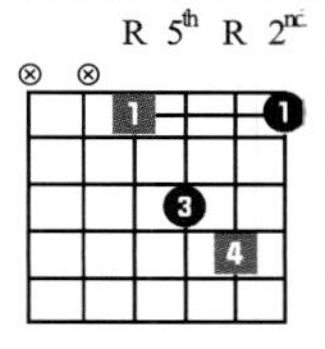
3	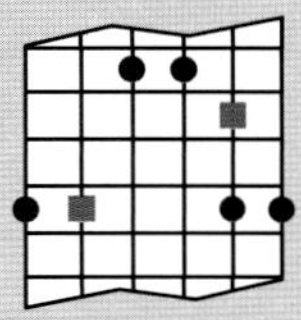	5th R 2nd 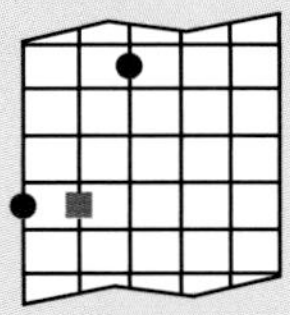	R 2nd 5th 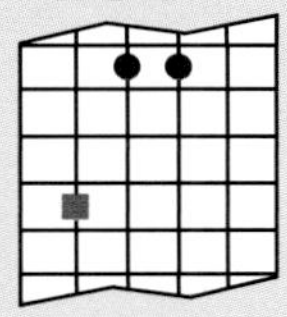	2nd 5th R 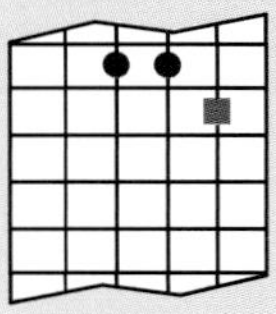		R 2nd 5th R 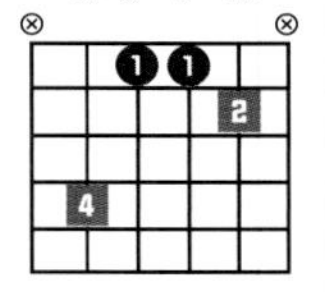
4	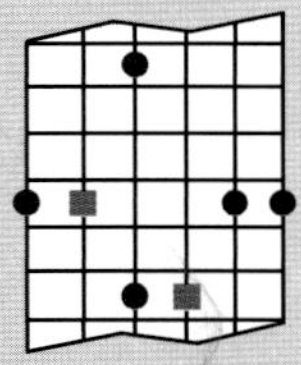	5th R 2nd 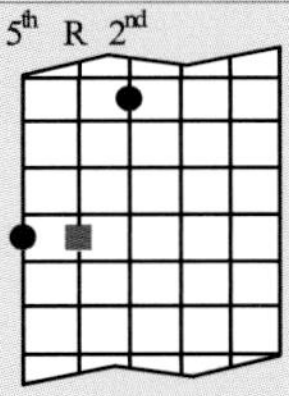		5th R 2nd 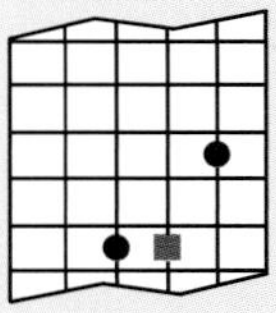	R 2nd 5th 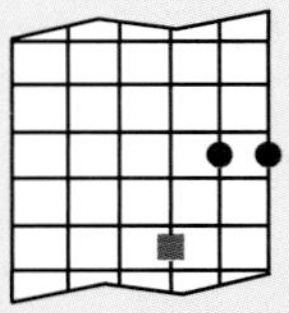	5th R 5th R 2nd 5th 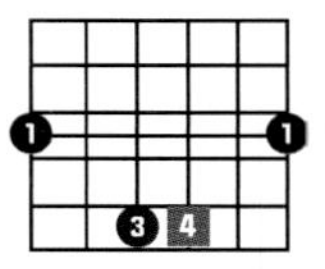
5	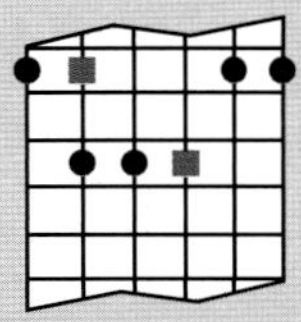		2nd 5th R 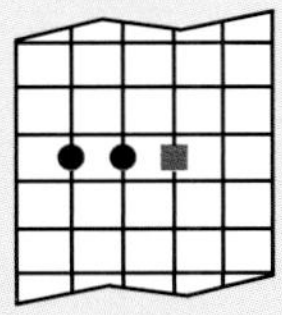	5th R 2nd 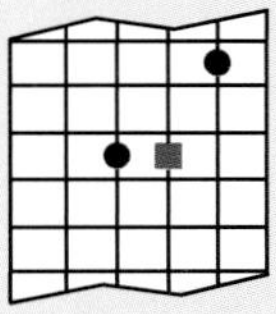	R 2nd 5th 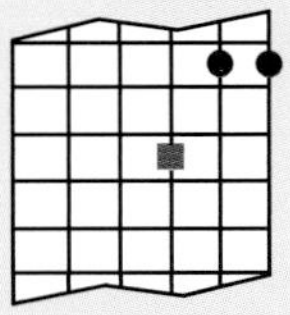	R 5th R 2nd 5th 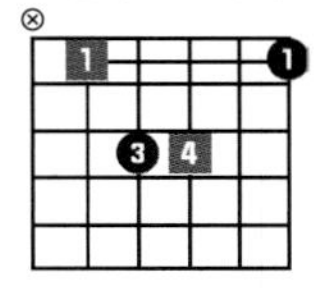
6	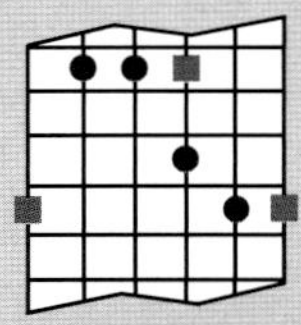	R 2nd 5th 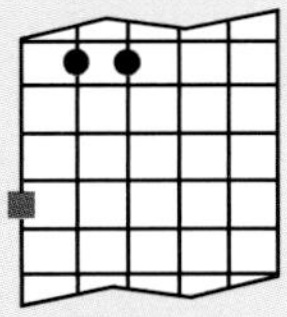	2nd 5th R 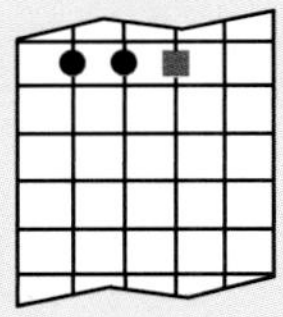		2nd 5th R 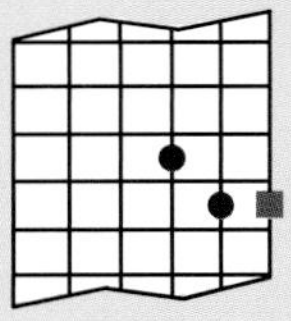	
7	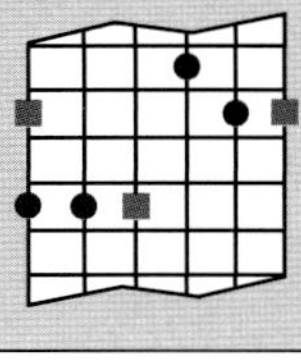	2nd 5th R 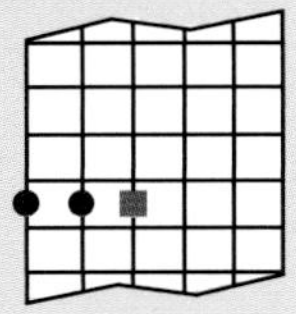	5th R 2nd 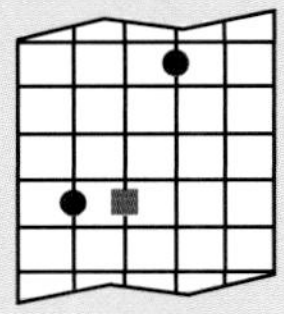	R 2nd 5th 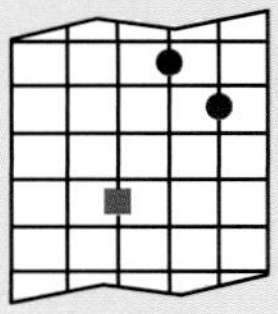	2nd 5th R 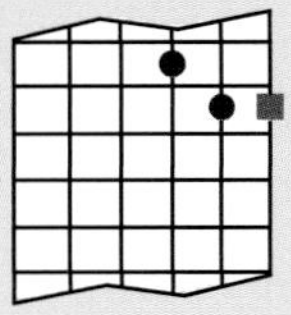	5th R 2nd 5th 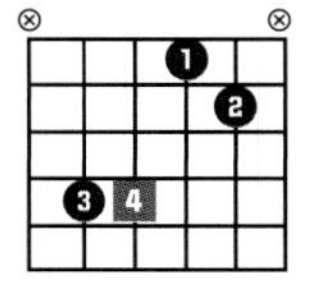

Sus4 Triad Study

	Sus4 Triadic Patterns	3-Strings Sus4 Triads				Sus4 Chords
		Strings 6, 5, 4	Strings 5, 4, 3	Strings 4, 3, 2	Strings 3, 2, 1	
1		4th 5th R	5th R 4th	R 4th 5th	4th 5th R	R 4th 5th R
2		4th 5th R	5th R 4th		5th R 4th	R 5th R 4th
3		5th R 4th	R 4th 5th	4th 5th R	5th R 4th	R 4th 5th R
4		5th R 4th				
5		5th R 4th		5th R 4th	R 4th 5th	R 5th R 4th
6		R 4th 5th	4th 5th R	5th R 4th		R 5th R 4th
7			5th R 4th	R 4th 5th	4th 5th R	R 5th R 4th 5th R